Ditch the Clock

Using Your

Attention Mindset

to Get Things Done

Felicity Edmond

Copyright © 2021 by Felicity Edmond.

All rights reserved. This book is designed to provide competent and reliable information regarding the subject matter covered. However, it is sold with the understanding that the author and publisher are not engaged in rendering medical, legal, or other professional advice or services. If medical, legal, or other expert assistance is required, the services of a professional should be sought. The author and publisher specifically disclaim any liability that is incurred from the use or application of the contents of this book.

No part of this book may be reproduced, distributed, stored in retrieval systems, or transmitted by any means, electronic, mechanical, photocopying, recorded, or otherwise, without written permission in writing from the publisher except in the case of brief quotations embodied in critical articles or reviews.

Table of Contents

Introduction 6

Chapter 1 Why We Should Bomb Time Management 11

The Debate: Giving Time Management the Flick 11

What consumes your attention? 21

    Types of attention 22

Chapter 2 The Brain's Superpower 28

Extraordinary Minds 28

    Different brain states you could experience 39

    How to nourish your brain to activate your attention 41

Chapter 3 Brain Fog 52

Slow Down: Thick Fog Ahead 52

    Eat a healthy breakfast 54

    Physical exercise 57

    Recall dreams 57

    Take a cold shower 59

    Declutter your space and mind 60

    Activate your goals 63

Chapter 4 Sleep 67

Rock-A-Bye Baby 67

    Stages of sleep 70

    Consequences of sleep deprivation 72

Practical ways to improve your sleep habits to activate your attention 75

Chapter 5 Motivation/Purpose 84

Defining Your Why 84

Chapter 6 Focus 100

Clear Vision 100

How to focus to activate your attention 107

Measure results 111

Pay attention to the process rather than the event 113

How to adjust your thinking to activate your attention 120

Chapter 7 Flow 126

Going With the Flow.. 126

How to get in a state of flow to activate your attention 132

Chapter 8 Procrastination 144

Should I, or Shouldn't I?... 144

Why do you Procrastinate?... 147

How to close the gap to activate your attention 149

Reclaim your responsibility... 149

Establish a routine 149

Share your commitments 150

Stop worrying.. 151

Chapter 9 The Spiritual Energy Superpower 155

Spiritual Energy Superpowers **155**
    Feeling a sense of connection 159
    Expanding your intuition 160
    Manifest synchronicity in life 162

Chapter 10 Behavioral Learning *178*

Learning Toolbox **178**
    Check how ready you are 180
    Is it required? 181
    How best do you learn? 181
    Get the right support 181
    Start small 182
    Skills you can learn to improve your productivity 183
    Decision-making 187
    Delegating 188
    Goal setting 192

Chapter 11 Instilling Good Habits *196*

Force of Habit **196**
    Limit technology 201
    Determine when you are most productive 201
    Break tasks into bite-size chunks 203

Conclusion *206*

Bibliography *210*

Introduction

Several years ago, I thought my running capabilities were limited to only chasing a ball when playing on the soccer field. My knees had cartilage damage, my weight was heavy, and my stamina was poor. I told myself that I couldn't run. To me, just running was boring and a waste of my time–after all, I had "better things to do." It was not until the beginning of 2020 that all changed.

My soccer friends had a premature sickly baby named Jay. They approached our soccer team to see whether we could help raise money for the maternity hospital to buy some special needs equipment they so desperately needed. The way they intended to raise the money was through sponsorship running a half marathon and they wanted us to run with them. What a dilemma! I so wanted to help but God knows I couldn't run ANY length, let alone a half marathon! I was 55 years old! I gave it some thought; I didn't want to let them down so I decided to give it a go. Don't try, don't get!

I started slowly. five kilometers, six days a week, 100 meters run, 100 meters walk, and slowly progressed to longer running distances and shorter walking distances. It was a daily commitment and a slow and steady progression. I concentrated on my why: why I was doing this, how I was engaging in the tasks, and building my capability. I did not concentrate on the time it took nor what I was doing with my time. Now, I am as productive as ever! I love it that I have achieved a new skill, that I have lost 18 kilograms, and that I now feel fit as a fiddle!

Just like you, I try to balance every aspect of my life. How many times have you told yourself you will get things done tomorrow? Perhaps you have promised yourself that you will get on top of things just in time. You have pushed your dreams, goals, and aspirations to tomorrow. But has tomorrow arrived yet?

Does it all have to do with time? Many of us struggle with time management. We think that if only we can manage time, we can be as productive as ever. Often, we think time management is the silver bullet if only we plan our time right, we can grow our businesses, spend more quality time with our family, or start doing the things we love and have been putting off for a long time.

No matter how hard you try to manage your time, it is never going to work! Instead of time management being *the solution*, it is *a problem*. Desire vs resistance. It is turning you into a stressed-out and unproductive human. Time management suggests that by eliminating all sources of distractions and scheduling how to distribute your time between your selected actions, you can increase your productivity. But how has that worked out for you?

Since you shut the door to your office, have people stopped interrupting you? Have you stopped interrupting yourself? Has your to-do list stopped you from getting sucked into social media?

So what's the alternative? For the past couple of years, I have learned that attention management offers the perfect alternative. It gets you to be thoughtful of the timing of all those distractions. It makes you realize that you can make progress in small intervals. To be more productive, quit analyzing how you spend your time. You cannot change the amount of time you have in any one day. Everybody has 24 hours in a day. Instead, focus on what consumes your attention. You want to be able to check off items on your to-do list with ease and grace, create an uplifting and fulfilling life, and build a balance across your home, family, and business life. I love what William James, author of *The Principles of Psychology*, once said, "*My experience is what I agree to attend to.*" In other words, what you choose to focus your attention on will determine the kind of life you live. To control your life, you must control your attention.

Look around you. You will notice that most of our experiences are blended. You can work anywhere: home, beach, plane, or train and still watch your kids from a nanny cam. Or, like me, you can run while listening to a podcast.

In this book, you will learn that your time is better spent paying attention to the things that truly matter—the ones that give you results. You will learn how to control distractions, stay present in the moment, and understand how your brain, sleep, motivation, focus, flow, and spiritual energy connect so that you can unleash your inner potential. You will learn how to become intentional rather than reactive and recognize when your focus is drifting away so you can pull it back on the things you choose to attend to. Instead of allowing distractions to drag you behind into postponing things, you will understand your goals, dreams, priorities, and aspirations and focus on them at any given time. Attention management goes beyond checking off your to-do list. It is about creating a life you choose.

Perhaps you are wondering, *"Why don't I just have the experiences I want to have? How do I create the life I most want to lead? Why is there a painful bridge between the self I aspire to be and how I spend my time?"*

Read on to find out.

Chapter 1 Why We Should Bomb Time Management

The Debate: Giving Time Management the Flick

When we increase our awareness, time adjusts to us, not the other way around

—Deepak Chopra.

Gladys, a research scientist with one of the world's most reputable research organizations, shared her story on her issues with time management with me. As a PhD student, she was used to long working hours in the laboratory and studying late at night. It was finally time for her to write her doctoral thesis of her original research she was performing. Each morning, she would wake up with a to-do list to go about her research paper writing. She would sit in the library for hours, her mind wandering about everything: what and where she was going to publish, the words to use, the people passing by, her graduation party, finding a new job, and so much more. She was distracted and couldn't write a single sentence. Days turned into weeks and weeks into months, but still no progress on her thesis. What was the problem? Her attention was on all the wrong things.

Time management

Time management refers to our ability to plan out our day, week, and month by scheduling time, prioritizing tasks, and trying as much as we can to be productive. The concept of time management is rooted in business. The 19th century Industrial Revolution paved way for people to create new relationships with time. Factory time demanded punctuality and workers had to learn how to live by the clock. Even schools became a place that prepared students to be good factory workers who "kept time." In other words, productivity was rooted on punctuality, hence the saying by Benjamin Franklin, *"Time is money"*.

Humans always search for better and efficient ways to get things done. It wasn't until the early 1900s that Frederick Winslow Taylor, the father of scientific management and author of *The Principles of Scientific Management, in 1911*, took a purposeful and scientific approach to doing things faster and with less effort. It all started as a quest to increase productivity in factories by focusing on employee efficiency. It quickly spread to the office and finally the home environment. Taylor found one best way to get things done–tools and standardized methods that effectively managed time.

Today, when people think of time management, the first thing that comes to mind is wasting less of it on things we want to do so that we spend most of it doing the things we have to do. In a nutshell, it is coined as a set of skills like goal setting, prioritizing, planning, scheduling, delegating, and decision-making. The theory is that once we master these skills, we become more organized, efficient, and happier.

The basics of time management are to plan ahead, prioritize tasks, eliminate distractions, and avoid multitasking. However, whether you use apps or an old pen and paper, the most effective way to manage time is to assess how you currently use the time you have, and then decide where to make changes.

The intentions and cons of time management

Intentions

- Produce better work
- Deliver work on time
- Become efficient
- Boost confidence
- Encourages multitasking

Cons

- Time cannot be controlled regardless of what we do
- Unclear targets
- Leads to fatigue because of predictive behavior
- Makes it difficult to say "No"
- Opens doors to obstacles, disruptions, and arguments
- The obsession of doing things right contributes to inactivity and stagnation
- Brings fatigue and stress
- Too much planning and too little action

Attention management

Attention management entails examining how much focus you give to a particular task. The whole point of attention management is to ensure that your focus is directed toward the things that truly matter—urgent, important, or both—without allowing less relevant things to get in the way.

Fundamentally, our attention is limited by the brain's processing power. The information theory argues that the human conscious mind has a processing capacity of 120 bits/second. To listen to someone speaking, we need at least 60 bits/second of processing power. This means that we can barely understand a thing when two or more people are speaking. German physiologist, Manfred Zimmermann, argues that the human sensory system can pick up information at a higher rate:

- The eye picks up 10 million bits/second
- The skin picks up 1 million bits/second
- Aural channel picks up 100,000 bits/second

The intentions and cons of attention management

Intentions

- Produces high quality results
- More fluid
- More flexible
- Harnesses a collection of behaviors, such as focus, concentration, mindfulness, presence, and flow
- Encourages single tasking

Cons

- Social interaction overload
- Information overload, hence mental fatigue
- Interruptions

That said, Levitin (2015) estimates that the daily information input of an average American was five times higher in 2011 compared to 1986. In other words, attention management is the most important skill in this time and age. With the advent of technology, internet, and communication devices, time management is no longer a guarantee of productivity and good performance. Allocating time to perform a task does not necessarily mean that it will capture your attention, especially when you are constantly distracted or interrupted. You can't actually create more time for yourself. Time management serves as a responsible steward of the time you have available to you. What you can control is your attention, hence attention management.

This is why you need to stop worrying about time management and instead focus on attention management!

You cannot control how you use the time available to you every day. Ultimately, time is not something anyone can harness. It is the reason many experts and leaders have shifted their focus to attention management.

How many times have you woken up early and told yourself you were going to get a report ready by noon? Just as you get started on the report, you hear a *ding!*– a recent email that steals your attention. You tell yourself that you need to answer it before you can get back to writing your report. You open your email, and you find several emails awaiting your response, and you decide, "What the hell, I might as well answer them now!" Half-way through the emails, you find one with a link to an article you need to review and send back. You start reading it, and by the time you are done, you realize it is 1.00 p.m.!

You start panicking and scolding yourself, but you cannot turn back the clock or pause time so you can make up for the hour you have lost.

So, what can you do?

You can reframe your mindset on productivity and how you can achieve it. Instead of trying hard to keep up with time, you can choose what, when, and how you focus on the tasks at hand.

Today, there are several tools–apps, organizers, and diaries–that claim to help us manage our time well. Often, when we first use these tools, they seem to help us. But after some time, you realize that something in that system does not work! You can estimate how long a task will take you to complete, but what you will never do is calculate time. We all perceive time differently. It is more like an inner experience. Unfortunately, the experience here is not all that matters. Other PhD research scientists like Gladys had manuscripts to write too, but in the end, each one of them spent a different amount of time to get it done.

Why is that the case?

It all depends on what you choose to focus your attention on.

Time, in itself, is a very abstract concept. Yes, the concept of time management has instrumental elements like setting goals, creating a to-do list, and prioritizing tasks, but you cannot slow it down or speed it up. In short, time is not manageable. Perhaps it worked in the pre-digital age, but its suggestions and strategies don't work for this digital world.

Today, we are faced with constant distraction every moment of every day. We try the best to stay focused on priorities amid all the distractions, both internal and external. Thoughts are growing on our to-do list, incoming emails, phone calls, text messages, notifications, colleagues, family, and so much more that call for our attention. When driving and speaking on the phone, attention is being switched between visual and auditory input, which constricts recognition of what is most important. As such, a driver cannot effectively react to a car braking in front of them or comprehend all the roadside billboards.

To determine the most important information, the brain must employ mental filters. Until you can manage your attention amid all these distractions, time management will not help you!

Stephen Covey, author of *"The 7 Habits of Highly Effective People,"* once said, "*The key is not to prioritize what's on your schedule but to schedule your priorities.*" You must realize that you don't need to buy into living your life within a time frame 24 hours a day, seven days a week, four weeks a month, 12 months in a year. If you fix yourself within these time frames, you are setting limitations in your mind. Your mind and body don't care what day of the week it is. All your body, mind, and soul care about is your energy, how you feel, and what you wish to attend to.

Take a minute to think about what you want to get done. You will realize that they are things you could have done or started doing already. It is also possible you think that you don't have enough time to get everything done. You have not done those things because you don't have enough time, but instead, you lacked attention and energy for them. To improve your productivity, you must quit trying to manage time and start focusing on something you can control—your attention!

What consumes your attention?

You become what you give your attention to

—Epictetus.

Today, attention is the most sought-after commodity. Everything around you is fighting for your attention. If you give it your attention, that thing has you: what you watch, read, or spend time with. In other words, everything that consumes our attention shapes who we become. If you choose to have a negative mindset, everything you see and do will be colored negative—garbage in, garbage out.

It is not just the apparent garbage you must guard yourself against. What matters is that you view attention as a finite resource that seeks your reservation so that you don't end up throwing away your attention on silent killers you persistently focus on instead of maximizing it in life-giving tasks. In other words, you must choose between being a master of your attention or getting swept away by the forces that fight it.

Perhaps you have heard people say, "I can't seem to pay attention. I'm sorry, I didn't hear what you said because I was not paying attention."

The most important question we should ask is, "Where on earth is all that attention going when it could serve us?"

Types of attention

Attention is not constant! You can change your attention span and intention depending on the situation. During your everyday activities, there are different types of attention. The kind you choose will depend on the circumstances and needs at that moment.

Type 1: Sustained attention

If you are continuously focusing on a specific task without distraction of any kind, it is called sustained attention. Whenever you hear the word "focus," "concentration," or "attention," the chances are that you think of sustained attention. For instance, when you are reading a book, listening to a lecture, or playing a video game, you need sustained attention.

It is hard to maintain this kind of attention for a long duration without getting distracted. At one time, you are intensely focused on the task at hand, and at the other, your attention lapses. The only difference here is that you can gently pull back your attention to the task at hand.

Type 2: Selective attention

Whenever there are various factors/stimuli present, you need to choose the one you want—hence selective attention. Every day, you are probably exposed to various environmental factors. However, the brain responds by choosing only one factor to focus on. For instance, if you study in a noisy room, your brain will choose one thing to focus on—studies.

Types 3: Alternating attention

This is mental flexibility that allows one to shift their attention between tasks with different cognitive requirements. Here, your brain will need to alternate attention back and forth between two tasks that call for engagement from different parts of the brain. For instance, when you are running and listening to a podcast or cooking while helping out your little ones with their homework.

Type 4: Divided attention

This refers to the ability to process two or more responses–aka multitasking simultaneously. For instance, you can be checking your emails during a meeting or dressing for work while speaking on the phone.

Most people tend to confuse alternating attention and divided attention, but they are different. You don't change from one task to another with divided attention, but instead, you perform both simultaneously. In other words, you are splitting your attention between the tasks at hand.

While most people boast of having the ability to multitask, it is humanly impossible to focus on more than one task simultaneously. The brain can only process one task at any given time. This explains why you cannot text and drive at the same time! The only reason you can use divided attention is because of muscle memory or habit. It is what allows you to read music while playing an instrument or drive while listening to music. However, the reality is that you are not focusing on both tasks simultaneously but doing the tasks without conscious effort.

Key Takeaway Points

- Time management is a problem, not a solution. You cannot slow time or speed it up-time is not manageable
- Time management says eliminate distractions, but time management will not help you until you can manage your attention amid all these distractions
- You are the one that decides who gets your attention, how it impacts you consciously, and whether it is worth it

- Every idea you consume shapes who you become, and that eventually becomes your world
- There are different types of attention: selective, sustained, alternating, and divided. The kind you choose will depend on the circumstances and needs at that moment
- To build your attention and learn the art of focusing, you must understand the power of focus and then establish the right environment, habits, and mindsets you wish to promote
- The most important thing is not how you use time but the intensity of your focus. If you increase your attention's intensity, you can get a lot done in minimal time
- To increase your attention span and stay focused, you must measure results and pay attention to the process rather than the event
- If you want to be more productive, don't analyze how you spend your time; pay attention to what consumes your attention

You don't get results by focusing on results. You get results by focusing on the actions that produce results

—Mike Hawkins.

Chapter 2 The Brain's Superpower

Extraordinary Minds

I own a cat, and perhaps you do too. And just like every other cat owner around the world, I am amazed by these animals' cunning plans, whether it is avoiding baths or trying to find food. But I am not here to discuss that. It's their brain's superpower that captivates me. These little creatures can process and apply information in incredible ways. By just observing what you do, they can repeat your actions and behaviors, hence the phrase "copycat."

The most exceptional cat I know observed her master teach children to play piano and developed this exceptional skill. After keen observation, she perched herself up at the piano and started tapping the keys with her paws, just like the children did.

What did she do? She watched, learned, practiced and applied her attention and focus to playing piano. Eventually, she was able to do what her master and students were doing.

That is an extraordinary mind right there!

Imagine if you attended a friend's graduation party. There are hundreds of people there, and you are trying to pick their face in a crowd. Doing this is such a complicated task. The brain must start by retrieving the memory of your friend's face, hold it in place as your eyes scan through the crowd, and pay close attention to finding a match.

Without focused attention, no amount of time will help you pick out your friend from a crowd!

According to a study conducted by neuroscientists Baldauf and Desimone (2014) at Massachusetts Institute of Technology (MIT), the brain achieves this kind of attention on objects by tapping into the power of the inferior frontal junction, the part of the brain located between the frontal sulcus and precentral sulcus. The human brain is indeed complex, but it is also magnificent. It is made up of several parts that each have a specific function:

- **The cerebrum:** The cerebrum is the largest part of the brain. It comprises the left and right hemispheres. The main role of this part of the brain is to interpret vision, touch, hearing, reasoning, learning, emotions, and fine control of movements

- **The cerebellum:** The cerebellum is located below the cerebrum. It is responsible for coordinating muscle movements, balance, and posture

- **The brainstem:** The brainstem connects the cerebrum and the cerebellum to the spinal cord. Its role is to perform various automatic functions like heart rate, breathing, wake and sleep cycles, body temperature, swallowing, sneezing, vomiting, and coughing

In short, the brain controls how you talk, eat, walk, and balance. It regulates your heart rate, breathing, and blood circulation. It is why you can speak, perceive, process, and recall information. Your brain controls how you make decisions and feel emotions.

Do all our brains function the same?

Every brain is unique, constantly evolving, and sensitive to our surroundings.

The brain weighs at least 3 pounds (about 1.35 kilograms), which makes about 2% of the human body weight. It comprises 100 billion neurons and takes up approximately 20% of the body's overall energy.

Perhaps you have heard people ask you whether you use more of your right brain or left brain. It is because the brain has two hemispheres: the right and the left hemispheres. These two sides of the brain look alike, but they play different roles and process information differently.

According to research conducted by Roger W. Sperry – an American neuropsychologist, neurobiologist and Nobel Prize Winner for his split-brain research–left brained people tend to be analytical and methodical in their thinking and the right-brained people tend to be more creative and artistic.

The left brain is often referred to as the digital brain because it is orderly, verbal, analytical, and better in computation, reading, and writing. The brain's right side is often termed the analog brain because it is more visual, intuitive, less organized, but more creative.

Perhaps you are wondering, "Is it possible that we have a dominant brain just like we have a dominant hand?"

There is no scientific proof that this theory holds water. Incidental findings in magnetic resonance imaging (MRI) brain research (Nelson, 2008) revealed that the brain does not necessarily favor one side. The neural networks on one side of the brain are not necessarily stronger than those on the other side.

Despite the differences in roles, they don't work independently of each other. They are interconnected by nerve fibers, hence creating an information highway. You don't use one side of the brain at a time. No matter what task you are performing, you receive input from both sides of the brain. Your tastes, personality, and learning styles don't necessarily classify you as left- or right-brained.

The brain continually reorganizes itself to adapt to change—both physical and psychological. You have heard people say you exercise your body muscles or lose them! The same applies to the brain. Your brain can continually develop and change throughout life.

You have to learn to stimulate your mind continually to keep it sharp for longer.

As we grow older, our brain changes. A study on the effects of aging and the brain (Peters, 2006) revealed that the brain shrinks by 5% per decade after we reach the age of 40. The rate of brain atrophy accelerates from 70 with an increased risk of stroke and Alzheimer's disease. With this degeneration, we tend to lose focus and struggle with planning and memory.

But why is it that some people still function normally even when they experience dementia? What is it about their brains that allow them to function effectively?

Cognitive reserve!

According to Erickson et al.,(2011), one's cognitive reserve can be maintained by life-long mental stimulation and nourishment of the brain. This does not change your IQ, but various mental activities in your daily life will challenge your brain and help you sustain your cognitive reserve. The trick is to continually exercise the brain so that it can compensate for age-related changes or disease. This is why mentally demanding occupations, education, and high-level social interactions can make one resilient to cognitive decline.

Perhaps you are reading this and wondering whether it is too late to increase your brain plasticity and boost your cognitive reserve?

The short answer is no!

The more you exercise your brain—intellectually, physically, and socially—the lesser the likelihood of depleting the mental reserves. If you don't use your brain, you will lose it.

Here's how the brain processes attention.

The brain is considered a powerful organ that can process loads of information. It is the role of your brain to control your behavior based on how you shape it. In other words, the brain can rewire neural connections that strengthen certain habits while weakening others. That said, it is susceptible to distractions. With its limited cognitive control, it can affect your goals and abilities to fight distractions.

Often, you have a specific goal in mind, but then something comes up and stands in the way of you completing the goal successfully. Distraction obstructs another process, both internal and external. For instance, when you have random thoughts bothering you throughout the day, that is an internal distraction. On the other hand, when you have your phone ringing nonstop, or colleagues knocking on your door with questions, they are external distractions. While you may want to ignore these distractions to achieve your goals, what stands out is winning against them or letting them win against you.

But why do they happen in the first place?

You make a conscious decision to engage them!

When you take on more than one task at a time, you are hurting your energy. You must understand that those various tasks have different goals and taking them on simultaneously is choosing to fail at all of them. According to research, the critical circuitry in the prefrontal cortex is in a state of synchrony when your focus is sharp, making it easier to attend to a task. In other words, when you pay attention to the task at hand, the brain maps the information you already know to what you intend to learn.

When your brain senses details that are not worth paying attention to, it automatically filters them.

But why is it increasingly difficult to pay attention to what truly matters?

The key lies in establishing a healthy balance. If you choose to get sucked into social media drama, the chances are that you will have very little energy to participate in the real world. Most people are overconsumed with other people's lives that they get less satisfied in their own. While there is nothing wrong with keeping up with the news, too much of it tends to make us anxious, skeptical, and out of control of our feelings. The remedy to this is taking back the control of our attention. You are the one that decides who gets your attention, how it impacts you–consciously–and whether it is worth it. If it doesn't serve you, you move on!

I like what Albert Einstein said, "The world as we have created it is a process of our thinking. You cannot change it without changing your thinking."

You must change the inputs—the things you give your attention to. Every idea you consume shapes who you become, and that eventually becomes your world.

So, are you comfortable with the things that shape you and your world? Does everything you focus your energy on echo a world you are proud to live in? There are only two ways you can live your life: as a mindless consumer or an engaged player. The longer you see something, the more you crave it. The more you engage in something, the harder it gets to see yourself outside of that thing. You will constantly compare yourself to it, feel less than it, crave it, fear it, be inspired or debilitated by it. To be productive in everything you do, you must be willing to become the person that wants more for their attention. As Epictetus said, "You must ensure that what you are paying attention to is worth becoming". You have to learn to be stingy with your attention. The best way to do this is by guarding your mind and eyes, knowing at the back of your mind that just somewhere around the corner, something wants that attention.

Back to the distractions: how do you manage them?

Well, the key is to identify obstacles!

Just so we are clear, not all distractions are equal: there are actual and perceived distractions. We are quite familiar with the former, but the latter tends to go unrecognized. Most of the time, even when there are no distractions around us, we tend to distract ourselves by expecting them. The problem with this is that they add up fast, impact the tasks on our to-do list, and leave us feeling unproductive.

Now, to manage your attention, let us imagine it as something you keep in your bank account. Each time you choose something to focus on, you pay for it. Soon enough, you will run out of it, and you will need to rejuvenate it. By taking on an exciting task and attempting to complete a challenging one after, chances are that you will not complete it because your attention is likely to have drained out. This means you should start with complex tasks first and then reward yourself with tasks you like later. The point here is to keep track of your attention residue!

Perhaps you are wondering, *"What is this attention residue anyway?"*

When you switch your attention from one task to another and back again, there is a cost you pay. The switching creates an attention residue that lowers your cognitive capacity for a given time before it clears. This means that you need to rejuvenate yourself and refill your attention stores constantly.

When you pay attention to a task, you are operating in a focused mode. The brain gathers lots of energy, sets up neural connections, and permits tasks. However, when you are not paying attention to any task, your brain is in a diffuse mode–it is lost in thought, sleep, walk, relaxation, etc. Just like life, it is vital to strike a balance between these two modes. Striking a balance can be enriching to life in the long run. Instead of allotting time to everything that comes your way, seek out those that matter to you and focus your attention on them. Time will fly as always, but it will be pleasant this time and worth it.

Different brain states you could experience

The brain state you experience depends on the brainwave, which measures the activity happening within your brain. The brain is an electrochemical organ that can power a light bulb. There are five different brainwaves, each of which is linked to a specific task and mental state:

- **Gamma waves:** Gamma waves are of highest frequency of all five. They are linked to insight, consciousness, and focus. When the brain is learning new information, storing memories, or concentrating, the gamma waves are generated

- **Beta waves:** Beta waves are what most people experience most of the time. They allow us to concentrate on complex tasks especially when we are reading writing or interacting. Unfortunately, when you are in this mind state, your energy, creativity, and emotional awareness can be easily drained

- **Alpha waves:** Alpha waves help us shift into a relaxed state when we get home after a long day. When you daydream, sleep, or enjoy a good read, the alpha waves are generated. However, if the brain experiences difficulties shifting from beta to alpha state, your risk of insomnia, OCD or anxiety is greatly increased.

- **Theta and Delta waves:** Theta and Delta waves are generated when we fall asleep. They promote deep restoration and dreamless slumber, like being in a hypnotic state. They are generated when operating on autopilot mode–like driving home using a familiar route or going about routine tasks like brushing teeth or taking a shower. In that state, your creativity flows because your behaviors are automatic and you can disconnect and just be.

How to nourish your brain to activate your attention

Drink plenty of water

The human body is composed of 70% water. The brain is one of the most important organs in the body and must be continually fueled. Out of the 70%, the brain accounts for 85% of this water. For the human brain to function, it must have abundant water access to keep the energy levels up and flush out toxins. Despite these facts, Dr. Alyson Goodman, expert epidemiologist from the U.S. Centers for Disease Control and Prevention (CDC), revealed that at least 43% of adults in the US don't drink enough water daily and 7 % of adults don't drink water at all!

Water gives the brain its electrical energy to function. In contrast to other body cells, brain cells require twice as much energy, and water effectively provides this energy. It is also vital for the production of hormones and neurotransmitters in the brain. Most of the brain's energy goes to the transmission of nerve signals. If your brain's water reserve is full, it will be more focused, creative, clear, and fast.

Ensuring that you stay hydrated throughout the day will help you think better and prevent the development of attention deficit disorders (ADD). Your brain does not have a way to store water for itself, hence the reason you must drink plenty of water throughout the day. When your body loses water more than you are replacing it, it impacts brain function and your attention.

Brain dehydration leads to a mental shut down – brain fog, poor attention, anger, headaches, depression, emotional instability, lack of mental clarity, etc. A meta-analysis (Wittbrodt & Millard-Stafford, 2018) of

413 research participants revealed that dehydration contributed to more than a 2% reduction in body mass, which significantly impaired executive function, attention, and motor coordination. Further, prolonged dehydration contributed to the shrinking of brain cells both in mass and size.

Water plays a critical role in supplying the brain with nutrients and getting rid of toxins. When you hydrate throughout the day, the exchange of nutrients and toxins becomes efficient, improving focus and mental alertness. It is recommended that you drink at least 12-16 ounces of water in the morning–which translates to 1.5 to 2 cups. Also, carry water in a bottle throughout the day to help keep the brain oxygenated, fueled, and brimming with energy.

Regular exercise

The more you work out, the stronger your brain gets. While there are no machines known to work the brain, engaging in general physical exercises can go a long way in raising your heart rate and boosting your brain memory. When you regularly exercise, you stimulate increased blood flow and supply of oxygen and nutrients to the brain, promoting optimal performance. Exercising also goes a long way in promoting the development of new cells and reinforcement of neural pathways. At least 30-45 minutes of movement every day triggers a series of memory-preserving benefits.

But how does exercise maximize your brainpower?

It increases the size of the hippocampus

As you age, this is the first part of the brain that gets dull. The hippocampus, located in the medial temporal lobes of the cerebrum, is responsible for verbal memory and learning. As you work out, the hippocampus volume grows, which makes the neurons denser and reinforces the neural connectivity. Regular exercise ensures that the brain stays focused, sharp, and protected from age-related cognitive decline. As little as 10 minutes of moderate exercise is enough to strengthen the cognitive power of the brain. Therefore, the next time you want to slack around, think about all the good your hippocampus stands to gain if you just decide to hit the gym.

It triggers the secretion of growth factors

The neural pathways and connections in your brain have a central role in your memory. For the brain to create new pathways and connections, it needs the action of growth factors. Regular exercising is one of the easiest ways to trigger the secretion of growth factors, like brain-derived neurotrophic factors (BNDF), in the brain. BNDF is a protein that preserves aging cells while promoting new ones, hence increasing nutrient and blood supply in the brain.

It slows the aging of the brain

Just because you are older does not mean your brain has to slow down. Remember what we said about cognitive reserves? To keep your focus sharp and memory preserved, exercising helps boost your cognitive reserve, keeping your brain healthy later in life. According to a study conducted by Gomez-Pinilla and Hillman (2013), people who exercised regularly in their youth had superior memory and cognitive skills than those who did not. Their scores in memory and cognitive skill tests matched those who were ten years younger than them.

That said, your brain is not picky on what exercises it requires to thrive. Any exercise that ramps up your blood circulation is a step in the right direction. Remember, your brain reaps benefits from increased heart rate and blood flow, and you can get this from cycling, running, soccer, tennis, and swimming. In other words, aerobic exercises and brain health go together because they increase blood flow and supply nutrients and oxygen to the brain. Additionally, anaerobic exercises like strength training and resistance movements are also great for your brain. Other low-impact workouts like tai chi, meditation, and yoga also go a long way in helping you strengthen your attention while lowering the levels of stress hormones in the body.

Good nutrition

For several decades, people have known that nutrition affects different parts of the body and the same applies to the brain. Research studies have shown that good nutrition goes a long way in boosting brain function and performance. When the brain is deprived of essential nutrients, there is an increased risk of cognitive decline. Most people ask whether there is a magic pill that ensures increased brainpower, but there is none. However, nutrition is a great strategy for improved mental function. Loading up on veggies, fruits, whole grains, and legumes is the best place to start. The most important nutrients for a healthy brain include:

Fats

According to research, at least 70% of the brain is fat. This does not mean you can eat all kinds of fats. The most useful fats are omega-3 fatty acids, which serve as essential building blocks of the brain. Omega-3 is found in large amounts in sardines, fish, walnuts, avocado, chia seeds, and flaxseeds. Healthy unsaturated fatty acids have been shown to lower beta-amyloid levels that commonly form damaging clumps in the brain among people with Alzheimer's disease.

On the other hand, saturated fats like those in fatty meat, butter, coconut oil, and whole-fat dairy products, are not good for your brain. The thing with these kinds of fats is that they oxidize over time and cause damage to cells.

Proteins

These are mainly building blocks of neurotransmitters, which transmit messages throughout the brain. You can get healthy proteins by consuming poultry, fish, eggs, legumes, and nuts. Eggs are rich in choline, which is known to boost brain function. You can also get more choline in cauliflower, peanuts, spinach, and beans.

Carbohydrates

They are known to supply the body and brain with fuel. What makes a real difference is the type and quality of the carbohydrates you consume. Complex carbs—with high fiber content like veggies, beans, whole grains, and beans—are recommended as they are loaded with antioxidants, vitamins, and minerals that fuel the brain and protect brain cells against oxidative stress. Additionally, complex carbs take longer to digest, which offers the brain a steady fuel supply compared to simple carbs. Carb foods with a high fiber content boost the gut microbiome, which is responsible for mood regulation.

Think of brain health like training for a marathon. Two days of good nutrition will not make up for the weeks you made bad dietary choices, but the good news is that it is never too late to start. Diet is a whole package and not just eating one or two superfoods. Make good dietary choices that support optimal brain health. Good nutrition should not feel like a struggle, but a lifestyle. You must be intentional in what you eat. What is good for your body is also great for your brain.

Key Takeaway Points

- Without focused attention, no amount of time will help you pick out your friend from a crowd
- Every brain is unique, constantly evolving, and sensitive to our surroundings
- The brain takes up approximately 20% of the body's overall energy
- The brain has two hemispheres: the right and the left hemispheres. These two sides of the brain look alike, but they play different roles and process information differently
- The left brain (digital brain) is orderly, verbal, analytical, and better in computation, reading, and writing

- The brain's right side (analog brain) is more visual, intuitive, less organized, but more creative
- No matter what task you are performing, you receive input from both sides of the brain
- The brain continually reorganizes itself to adapt to change, both physical and psychological
- The brain shrinks by 5% per decade after reaching the age of 40
- The rate of brain atrophy accelerates from 70 with an increased risk of stroke and Alzheimer's disease
- One's cognitive reserve can be maintained by life-long mental stimulation and nourishment of the brain
- The more you exercise your brain, intellectually, physically, and socially, the lesser the likelihood of depleting the mental reserves
- To nourish your brain:
    - Drink plenty of water
    - Engage in physical exercise
    - Eat right

Our minds influence the key activity of the brain, which then influences everything; perception, cognition, thoughts and feelings, personal relationships; they're all a projection of you

—Deepak Chopra.

Chapter 3 Brain Fog

Slow Down: Thick Fog Ahead

A couple of years ago, Martina walked into a supermarket to shop for household supplies. After a couple of minutes, she went over to the counter and paid for her supplies. The supermarket attendant helped get her shopping into the car and left. Martina got into the car, started the engine, and drove toward the exit. Having been a weekend, many people were shopping at the mall. At the exit was a long queue of vehicles waiting to leave. When Martina's turn came, she realized that she had not paid for parking and couldn't leave.

Perhaps after shopping, you forgot where you parked your car? Or even worse, took a taxi home thinking that you came in a taxi, only to realize that your car is parked at the supermarket's parking bay. Or maybe there are times when you read a passage a hundred times without absorbing anything you read.

We all have been in a situation where we experience momentary memory lapse. You feel like the world around you is spiraling fast. This is referred to as brain fog. It is not a disease but a state of chronic mental fatigue, lack of attention, and cognitive dysfunction. Often, a brain fog shows up in several ways where your head feels like it has been stuffed with sand. You know there is a power outage, but then you find yourself at the switch trying to turn on the lights. You find it hard to focus on the task at hand - conversations, writing, or reading. The decisions you normally make in a split second seem to be taking you a long time to process.

Simply put, you don't feel like yourself!

The symptoms vary from a lack of focus, chronic fatigue, forgetting things, to mental flatlining. Experiencing any of these symptoms can be mentally draining. It can feel like living in a dome and watching the world go by, and there is nothing you can do about it. You feel you should be at the top of your tasks, but for some reason, you are not. This is not something that affects the old or the sick alone—it affects everyone and anyone. If you have been experiencing this lately, know that you are not alone.

Brain health is vital to your emotional wellbeing and mental capacity. What you think and feel are intimately connected. To feel good, you must think good.

It can be a symptom of many things: sleep disorder, depression, nutrient deficiency, sugar-rush, bacterial growth, inactivity, poor diet, stress, etc.

Unlike the flu, this is not something you catch or ride out until the symptoms clear. It is your brain telling you there is something in your daily life that needs change. However, figuring this out is probably not at the top of your to-do list because you are not thinking straight in the first place.

So, what can you do to regain mental clarity?

Eat a healthy breakfast

You have probably heard people say breakfast is the most important meal of the day, and it is true. However, it is easy to skip breakfast with all the morning rush: preparing kids for school, getting ready for work, and house chores. We find ourselves giving excuses like, "I don't have time for breakfast, I have to get to work," or "Breakfast makes me hungrier!"

Think about it; will your car move if it doesn't have gasoline to start the engine? The same applies to the body—you need food for the brain to function well. Even if you are trying to lose weight, skipping breakfast is a recipe for missed goals. Breakfast will indeed make you hungrier because it activates metabolism, and that is a good thing! We all have busy schedules, but we still find time to do the little things in the morning, right? We are in a rush, but we take a shower, brush our teeth, and dress for work. So, why can't you spare a little time for breakfast?

Making breakfast part of your morning ritual is the way to go! It tells your brain that you are ready to focus on tasks that lie ahead of you. A healthy and balanced breakfast—like eggs and fiber-rich cereals—will keep you satisfied until your next meal. If you are on a weight loss program, taking breakfast will prevent you from overindulging in empty calorie snacks. It doesn't matter whether you sit at the table to have breakfast or grab it on the go, the most important thing is choosing to have breakfast.

A review study, published in the *Italian Journal of Pediatrics* in 2013, reveals that people who eat breakfast have improved cognitive function and performance, and better nutrient consumption, attention, and memory than those who don't. It is not enough to just have breakfast but to get the right nutrients the body and brain need. Eating a healthy and balanced breakfast interrupts the depletion of nutrients the body is constantly using while ensuring that the brain gets a constant nutrient supply. Lamport et al. (2014) found that there was improved attention and memory among adolescents who ate a low-glycemic breakfast–oatmeal, whole-grain bread, and other cereals with a high fiber content—compared to those who ate a high-glycemic breakfast or had no breakfast at all.

Think of breakfast as an opportunity to choose foods that are good for your brain–flaxseeds, cherries, blueberries, eggs, fruits, yogurt, cereals, etc. To make breakfast part of your morning ritual, here's what you need to do:

- Keep it simple
- Create a meal plan
- Plan for on-the-go breakfast
- Make a conscious commitment to eat breakfast

Physical exercise

With all that is going on in our lives and around us, it is easy to get stressed out. Each time you are stressed, your brain gets stressed, too. Stress hormones contribute to brain fog, which slows one's cognitive skills and dampens brainpower. Exercising serves as a potent tool in relaxing the mind: walking, jogging, or strength-training. Engaging in physical activity has been shown to lower the secretion of stress hormones, norepinephrine and cortisol, that cause the brain to worry and get anxious. It also triggers the release of feel-good hormones, endorphins which boost the mood and stimulate the hippocampus's growth.

Recall dreams

Mental clarity can start with recalling your dreams when you wake up in the morning. Have you thought about why dreams are important?

According to Sigmund Freud's–an Austrian neurologist and the founder of psychoanalysis – canonical text on The Interpretation of Dreams (1899), dreams are the keys to our unconscious mind. They play a key role as mental safety valves that allow us to experiment on what it might feel like acting on our impulses or emotions. The main role of dreams is to help in the storage of memories and things we have learned, eliminate unimportant stuff, and sort through complex feelings and thoughts. Dreaming helps the brain block stimuli that interfere with learning and memory.

But why remember your dreams?

Think of recalling your dreams as interacting with a toddler who is learning language. Just because the toddler cannot say things clearly does not mean they are ridiculous or useless. You simply focus on in the hope you will hear at least one word clearly.

The same applies to our dreams. When recalling dreams, you are learning how to listen to yourself, the non-linear language you speak. The trick is to set the intention to remember your dreams when you go to bed. Understand that your dreams are part of your creativity and intelligence. Realize that the only way you can build a relationship with anyone is if you focus your attention on them – what they are saying and not saying (non-verbal cues). When you focus on even the smallest dream fragments, you make it easy to reinforce these small bits, which encourages an increase in behavior. Write these bits down and try not to interpret them while writing. When you do this, you re-stimulate the emotional state associated with them, which loops back to your dream recall.

Don't get out of bed without triggering recall to avoid even the slightest distractions getting in the way of your attention.

Take a cold shower

The cold makes you go within

—Wim Hof.

According to Dr. Rhonda Patrick, Founder of My Fitness, taking a cold shower or cold shocking the body is key to activating and waking up the mind. When you take a cold shower, the brain triggers the release of norepinephrine hormone to the blood, which in turn calms us down and boosts attention, focus, and mood.

Declutter your space and mind

Look around you—your closet, office, home, and even your body. Are you surrounded with clutter? While cluttered spaces can be debilitating, the worst of all is the kind of clutter we keep in our minds. That feeling makes you drive on autopilot, forget important events, leave the water running, stumble over your words without making a point.

When you are caught up in your head, it can be impossible to focus. This causes us to lose connection with ourselves, the surroundings, and life. Mental clutter tends to pull us off center and interferes with our balance. What mental clutter is standing in the way of your mental focus? Perhaps it is information overload, expectations, procrastinating tasks, or negative feelings—like regret, shame, worry, anger, anxiety, and frustration—that are filling up your mind. Your attention has shifted to your *head-trash*.

You don't need all the junk. Imagine coming home to a messy kitchen —dirty dishes in the sink and all over the worktops, food spills on the floor, dirty kitchen towels, and so much more. Will you be motivated to cook? Let's flip the coin—you come home to a clean and tidy kitchen. Will you be motivated to cook?

A messy mind can do the same: dampen your focus, motivation, and productivity. Your mind is not built to split attention in too many directions. Perhaps you are wondering, *"How can I clear clutter I cannot see?"*

To declutter the mind, you must be intentional about where you want your attention to go and how you intend to spend your energy and time. When you work in a cluttered space, it is easy for the mind to get distracted on objects, colors, people, files, etc. Although you are not consciously thinking of the clutter, the subconscious mind is distracted by everything lying around. Organizing your workspace and closing all the "open tabs" in your mind helps reduce brain fog.

So, how do you do it?

- The first thing you must do is work on small tasks you have been putting off. If it doesn't take more than five minutes to complete, do it immediately. Then focus on bigger tasks by prioritizing them – in order of importance and urgency

- Clean up your physical space. When you are drowning in stuff, your imagination and creativity are impaired
- Let go of expectations that don't serve you–the *woulda, coulda, shoulda* stuff you have no control over so that you can see the good that lies before you. This does not mean tolerating situations of people that hurt us repeatedly. You can let go of something and distance yourself from them
- Filter the incoming thoughts. Instead of beating yourself up for the mistakes you made, choose to focus on what you did right. This way, your focus, and energy are not invested in negative self-talk but instead in brainstorming solutions
- Set boundaries on your relationships
- Take some downtime

We are all unique beings, and what might cause you brain fog might not apply to someone else. Your role is to find your solution, and that will take trial and error. Experiment with diet, get good sleep, hydrate, exercise, decompress, and check your overall health condition. The trick is to be proactive about adopting a brain-healthy lifestyle that promotes mental clarity. Trust me, no one cares about your brain as much as you do–

treat it as your priority and watch how that impacts your cognitive capacity.

Activate your goals

What goals do you wish to achieve? Are they exciting?

It's one thing to have SMART goals, but it is another that makes them exciting. Exciting goals help us focus. When you know why something works, you become more willing to embrace it, be more informed, and better at decision-making. The best way to get rid of your brain fog is to activate your dreams, passion, desires, and goals.

So, how does activating your goals improve your focus?

When your goal is clear and compelling, it helps mobilize your focus toward an actionable behavior. Setting goals should motivate you. If you are saving to buy a home, you can ask yourself how big you want the house to be, the neighborhood you wish to live in, and how soon you want the house. Having specific goals gives your mind a clue that triggers your attention and motivates you to start saving.

There are goals, passions, and dreams you have buried for far too long. You wanted to get your degree, start a business, lose weight, or buy a home or a car. Whatever your goals might have been, activating them naturally directs your attention toward the next step in the right direction. It forces your actions and behaviors to follow suit. There is a cheesy saying I like: "Whatever the mind believes the body achieves."

Progress can be addictive. The moment your attention is directed on your goals and your actions start bringing results, the brain releases dopamine, the feel-good hormone. Progress in your goals sustains momentum. In the same way, a snowball grows as it rolls down a hill, momentum works the same way. When you start seeing results in your weight loss, making profits from your business or saving the first fraction for your car, you are motivated to keep the momentum going.

You are not just activating your goals to achieve mental clarity but also promote self-mastery. Your goals build your character. Think of pursuing your goals as a money-maker. The moment you start achieving them, they build your efficacy, and you start seeing yourself as someone who can achieve anything.

Now, you know how to regain your mental clarity. The most important thing is that you become mindful of keeping the clutter out. Take a walk, jog, swim, do gardening, catch up with friends, limit social media, and whatever else will help keep your head clear. Don't be too hard on yourself if you feel you can't even sort your socks. What you need is to build your momentum, find that missing piece, and check which one of your ideas measure up to your overall life. If your mind is on the clear, there is nothing you cannot achieve—if you put your mind to it! You can certainly move from zero to hero, but you must get rid of clutter to make room for goals.

Key Takeaway Points

- Brain fog is not a disease but a state of chronic mental fatigue, lack of attention, and cognitive dysfunction
- The symptoms vary from a lack of focus, chronic fatigue, forgetting things, to mental flatlining

- Brain health is vital to your emotional wellbeing and mental capacity—to feel good, you must think good
- Eating a healthy and balanced breakfast interrupts the depletion of nutrients the body is constantly using while ensuring that the brain gets a constant nutrient supply
- To make breakfast part of your morning ritual:
    - Keep it simple
    - Create a meal plan
    - Plan for on-the-go breakfast
    - Make a conscious commitment to eat breakfast
- Exercising relaxes the mind. Walking, jogging, or strength-training lowers the secretion of stress hormones –norepinephrine and cortisol and triggers the release of feel-good hormones – endorphins
- Declutter the mind and be intentional on where you want your attention to go and how you intend to spend your energy and time

Chapter 4 Sleep

Rock-A-Bye Baby

Like most people, I juggle a lot of work every day, taking the kids to school and to their afterschool activities, doing house chores, working long hours, playing with my soccer team, exercising, getting prepared for the next day, and so much more. When I get home in the evening, I feel like I have been carrying a huge log on my shoulders all day. Don't get me wrong, I love what I do, but almost all the time I feel exhausted. If you are a runner like me, you know that there are additional challenges that accompany this sport even if you are doing it for fitness–injuries, performance fatigue, excessive sweat, high average heart rate, and so much more. All these activities make it even harder to get sleep at night, and when you are about to catch a few winks, the alarm goes off–it's time to get up.

This is a real struggle!

Every person has a unique sleep story. What is yours like? Do you feel sleep deprived? How many hours of sleep do you get at night? Have you made sleep a priority? Oh, I see, you still haven't.

Most people have not!

There are occasions when we sit in a class or meeting room half asleep. We try hard to pay attention to what is being discussed to no avail. Have you wondered why that is the case? A research study published in *Nature Neuroscience* (Yoo et al., 2007) revealed that just one night of sleep deprivation severely affects hippocampal activity, making it hard for one to focus, and worsens subsequent memory retention.

We have heard people boast about the crazy hours they work and how little sleep they get because they are "productive." This type of thinking is utterly misguided!

You must understand that sleep is not something you have, but instead, it is something you do. It refers to the mind and body's condition that recurs for several hours every night, where the nervous system is relatively inactive, the postural muscles are relaxed, the eyes are closed, and our consciousness is suspended. In short, sleep is an important part of our daily routine. But there is a difference between being in bed and getting quality sleep—enough of it. Just as food and water are essential for survival, so is sleep. Without sleep, your brain will not maintain important pathways that allow you to concentrate, learn, create memories, and respond quickly. It does not just affect the brain, but almost every other system in the body, like the lungs, heart, immune function, metabolism, and mood. A chronic lack of sleep increases the risk of developing such disorders as high blood pressure, depression, heart problems, obesity, and diabetes.

Most people think that sleep is a single state of mind when it is a complex set of brain processes supporting our psychological needs. Sleep deprivation severely affects our attention, which suggests that sleep is a key regulator of attention. For the brain to filter incoming stimuli based on relative salience, there must be coordinated synaptic activity across the brain.

Not only does sleep prepare the brain to encode new memories, but it also helps the brain consolidate and integrate new information. When you are trying to learn something, you need enough sleep to focus on tasks. When you are sleep-deprived, the attentional networks in the frontal and parietal lobes of the brain experience reduced activation.

Our daily experiences shape the way we perceive our surroundings. With selective attention, our awareness of certain things is heightened while awareness of others is dampened. During sleep, our perception tends to fade more broadly. This leaves us unaware of what is happening in the outside world. While these two perceptual states—sleep and attention—may seem like opposites, they play a central role in regulating our awareness, suggesting a deep connection between sleep and attention.

Stages of sleep

There are two basic types of sleep:

- Rapid eye movement (REM)
- Non-REM sleep

Each type of sleep is associated with specific brain waves and neural activity. When you sleep, you cycle through different REM and non-REM sleep stages several times at night, with longer and deeper REM cycles happening toward morning.

Stage 1

This is a non-REM sleep that involves a changeover from a state of wakefulness to sleep. During this time, you are in relatively light sleep. The heart rate, breathing, and eye movements are slow. The muscles are relaxed with twitching from time to time. Here, the brain waves are beginning to slow from daytime wakefulness patterns.

Stage 2

This is also a non-REM sleep period with light sleep as you transition to deeper sleep. Here, the heartbeat and breathing become even slower, and the muscles relax further. The eye movements stop, and the body temperatures drop. The brain wave activity is slower but is characterized by brief bursts of electrical activity. Most of your repeated sleep cycles are spent on this stage compared to other sleep stages.

Stage 3

This is a non-REM sleep where you are in a deep state of sleep. This is important in ensuring that when you get up, you are fully refreshed. It happens in longer periods during the first half of the night. The breathing and heart rates are at their lowest levels here. The muscles are relaxed, and if someone tries to wake you, it's going to take time. The brain waves are even slower.

REM sleep

This happens at least 90 minutes after you fall asleep. During this time, your eyes move rapidly from side to side behind the closed eyelids. The brain waves are closer to those of a wakeful state. The heart rate and breathing are faster and irregular—most of the dreaming is happening here, while some happen in non-REM sleep. Here, the arms and legs are temporarily paralyzed to not act out of your dreams. As you age, you sleep less in this stage.

Consequences of sleep deprivation

When you are sleep deprived, your reaction time is affected. Reaction time refers to the length of time it takes to respond to a stimulus. It is the event that comes before a response. Typically, it takes the brain 160—190 milliseconds to respond to a physical stimulus. While physical responses can happen within a blink of an eye, there are a series of processes in the brain.

When a ball is thrown at you, what happens? You catch the ball, right? But that is not all. The brain must recognize the ball, decide to respond, and send a signal through the spinal cord to the hands and fingers.

Our reactions vary based on many factors, some of which are outside our control, like age, type of stimuli (visual or auditory), or whether you are right- or left-handed. Others are within our control—like the level of physical fitness, level of fatigue, and presence of distraction.

So, how does a lack of sleep affect your reaction time?

According to the National Sleep Foundation guidelines, adults require between seven and nine hours of sleep every night. This is essential for optimal physical and mental function. Unfortunately, a survey, conducted by the Center for Disease Control in the District of Columbia and across all 50 states, reveals that at least a third of the American population gets less than six hours of sleep per night.

As your sleep debt accumulates, your reaction time increases. In other words, the more sleep you lose, the longer it takes to react to a stimulus. Bonnet and Arand

(2003) studied the clinical effects of sleep fragmentation and sleep deprivation. The research participants were allowed to sleep only five hours every night for seven days. As the days went by, the participants' reaction time increased as they accumulated sleep debt.

When you are under-slept, your body increasingly experiences a need for sleep, a need to stay awake and perform tasks. These competing needs get in the way of our attention from time to time and eventually lead to cognitive impairment and increased reaction time.

If you are behind the wheel of a vehicle, what happens when your reaction time increases? Most of the work we do requires sustained attention and a quick reflex. If your reaction time is increased, it can be particularly dangerous! The statistics given by The National Highway Traffic Safety Administration in the US (2009—2013) reveal that over 6,000 fatal crashes annually are because of drowsiness.

When you drive while sleep-deprived, it can make it difficult to navigate the road conditions quickly, and you may end up drifting from your lane. The brain cells are sluggish, and you become more forgetful and easily distracted. This makes it hard for the brain cells to effectively communicate, leading to temporary mental lapses that affect your visual perception and memory. You can barely think clearly or concentrate on tasks.

Practical ways to improve your sleep habits to activate your attention

Your bedroom

If you have trouble falling asleep and staying asleep throughout the night, your bedroom is the first place to look at. You need the right setting–clean, peaceful, and welcoming–to get a restful night. Most people unknowingly sleep in rooms that are not fit for purpose, which means your environment might be the key to a restless night.

Some of the tips that will help you create a space that encourages peaceful night sleep include:

- Make the room completely dark using curtains of blackout blinds

- Maintain ambient temperatures of between 16° and 18° C. When the room is too hot or too cold, it makes it hard to sleep
- Remember what we said about decluttering? A tidy room—clean, neat, and simple—means a tidy mind and a restful night's sleep
- Don't bring technology, phones, and TVs to the bedroom
- If there must be any technology in the bedroom, ensure your emitted bright screen light is off. These lights restrict the production of melatonin, the hormone that regulates your circadian rhythms—your asleep/awake rotations
- Don't treat your bedroom as an extension of the rest of the room. In other words, don't watch, eat, or work in the bedroom. If you treat it as a place for sleep and sex, your mind will do the same
- Bring in special touches like plants, family portraits, ornaments, and flowers to make it pleasant, peaceful, and relaxing
- Bring in scents that are naturally calming and relaxing, like geranium and lavender

Your bed

A comfortable bed is the foundation of a good night's sleep. Choose the right mattress that will encourage you to have a restful night, and save you from fatigue, and irritability throughout the day. If the mattress does not encourage a good sleeping posture, the chances are that you will not have a quality sleep because your body will suffer aches and pain.

Some tips to help you choose the right bed are:

- Put quality above the price
- Go for a mattress that offers you the right support – firm enough to support correct spinal alignment and conform to the body's contours
- Try the bed and mattress before you buy by spending at least 10—15 minutes in different positions
- Don't wait until the bed is completely worn out to change it. It is recommended that you change the bed every seven years

Your lifestyle

We live in a fast-paced time characterized by chaos, jams, and technology. From the time you get up, you switch on your brain with a smartphone. As the day progresses, we encounter even more triggers—emails, social media, TV, and radio—that add up to non-stop stimulation. It is the reason we complain "I can't sleep" and struggle to get out of bed in the morning. What you need is to adjust your lifestyle so that you can wind down and relax.

- The first thing is to maintain a regular bedtime routine and sleep pattern.
- Stay away from caffeine before bedtime.
- Try not to do any sporting activity before bedtime.
- Unplug from technology 30-60 minutes before bedtime
- Try not to consume too much fluid before bedtime.
- Try not to take naps during the day.

Diet

You probably have heard of the saying, "You are what you eat!"

As far as getting a restful night's sleep goes, what you eat and drink has effects. The best foods to eat include chicken, rice, cherries, and milk. You cannot eat curry and drink alcohol and expect to have a quality sleep. You need a diet that promotes the three chemicals of good sleep:

1. Serotonin,
2. Melatonin, and
3. Tryptophan.

1. **Serotonin:** Serotonin is a neurotransmitter commonly referred to as the body's happiness drug. It is found in the digestive system and blood platelets throughout the central nervous system (CNS). This neurotransmitter is made from tryptophan, which is found in diet. It is a hormone that boosts our positivity and relaxation for a good night's sleep, making us feel refreshed and energized. This is the energy you need to get going in the morning and get rid of the lethargy that might otherwise keep you in bed

2. **Melatonin**: – if you ask any sleep expert, they will tell you melatonin is the hormone of darkness. To kick-start the sleep cycle, it is important that you are in a dark environment, with the lights out and technology lights off. That shift from light to dark

sends a signal to the brain to secrete melatonin, which helps the body wind down to a sleep-ready state. In other words, without melatonin, it is impossible to achieve restful sleep

3. **Tryptophan:** This is an amino acid found in protein foods. Tryptophan is used in the body as a precursor for making serotonin and melatonin

You can get supplements over the counter too. Also, combine a protein and low-to-medium glycemic index carb that optimizes tryptophan levels in the body.

Changing your time to promote good sleep patterns will not happen overnight. Good things take time, and you need to be patient. The best place to start is by keeping a sleep diary to help keep track of your progress.

Exercise

Working out plays a key role in helping you get better sleep. Yes, exercising is not easy, and most of the time, the body will feel spent. However, it releases pent-up tension that banishes stress so that you can have a relaxed night. It lowers body temperatures to induce sleep. That said, it is best if you don't overdo it. Wearing yourself out physically will not induce sleep. You don't want to be extra alert when you should be sleeping.

When you work out, remind yourself why you are doing it—to be fit and healthy. If you exercise and still experience sleep problems, try changing the type of activities you do or the time you are doing them. Try yoga to reap its relaxation and sleep benefits. Walking and other moderate-aerobic exercises have also been shown to help one fall asleep fast.

The more you challenge your body every day, the easier it is to fall asleep. When you get up, you will be feeling recharged, rejuvenated, and energized. Getting quality sleep has been shown to improve mental clarity and brain function. With good sleep, you can stay focused, make good decisions, and efficiently process emotions. This is mainly because the brain had enough time to rest and prepare for the tasks that await. During sleep, the brain is at full capacity for sharpened cognitive skills and reinforced memory.

Key Takeaway Points

- Sleep deprivation severely affects hippocampal activity, making it hard for one to focus, and worsens subsequent memory retention
- Sleep is not something you have but instead, it is something you do
- Without sleep, your brain will not maintain important pathways that allow you to concentrate, learn, create memories, and respond quickly
- Not only does sleep prepare the brain to encode new memories, but it also helps the brain consolidate and integrate new information
- There are two basic types of sleep:
    - Rapid eye movement (REM)
    - Non-REM sleep
- When you sleep, you cycle through different REM and non-REM sleep stages several times at night, with longer and deeper REM cycles happening toward morning
- As your sleep debt accumulates, your body increasingly experiences a need for sleep, a need to stay awake and perform tasks—lead to cognitive impairment and increased reaction time

- Practical ways to improve your sleep habits:
    - You need the right setting–clean, peaceful, and welcoming–to get a restful night
    - A comfortable bed is the foundation of a good night's sleep
    - Adjust your lifestyle so that you can wind down and relax
    - You need a diet that promotes the three chemicals of good sleep: serotonin, melatonin, and tryptophan
    - Exercise releases pent-up tension that banishes stress so that you can have a relaxed night
- With good sleep, you can stay focused, make good decisions, and efficiently process emotions

Chapter 5 Motivation/Purpose

Defining Your Why

Take a minute to think about this: What gets you excited about what you do? Why is it important?

Several years ago, Matilda was living the dream. She had just completed her PhD, won a senior scientist job with a prestigious global research organization, owned a dream car, owned a dream house, and lived with her dream family.

But each morning she woke up, she felt like she was missing a part of her. She was not complete. She traveled the world for meetings and conferences, enjoyed good remuneration packages, but yet still felt miserable. While Matilda was successful and ran a $10 billion-dollar project with a dream team, she felt insignificant. She narrated, "I thought the feeling would eventually go away, and I would finally get back to enjoying every bit of my job, but that never happened."

Why wouldn't she quit?

She had a family to support, bills to pay, and a mortgage to service!

Just around that time, she watched the movie *The Lion King* that deeply impacted her life. The line where Mufasa spoke to Simba, saying, "Remember who you are. You are more than what you have become," specifically spoke to her. It was as if she has just woken up from a deep slumber.

It immediately dawned on her that she was more than all her achievements combined. Even though she had achieved her goals in life, somehow, she had lost the way. Like Simba, she felt like she had been running away from her true purpose. Even though she was living what most people consider "the ultimate dream," she knew her purpose was waiting for her however long it took.

Perhaps like Matilda, you have realized that the life you are living is not your true purpose. Yes, you are afraid to change–take the risk and get out of your comfort zone. Deep inside, you feel something is missing – you are not complete. You have achieved your goals, but yet something still needs to change. You may be scared of losing what you have built over the years.

What would you do if you knew you couldn't fail? What would you do without getting paid? What makes you feel alive and complete?

Matilda knew her calling was motivational coaching. She knew deep down that even if she did not get paid, she would wake up every morning to speak to someone and impact their lives. Coaching people to get out there, take risks, and achieve greatness made her come alive –what an irony, right?

Today, she has coached over 2,000 companies in over 50 countries. She has written motivational books that have changed lives across the world. She does what she loves and that makes her feel complete!

As long as I can remember, I feel I have had this great creative and spiritual force within me that is greater than faith, greater than ambition, greater than confidence, greater than determination, greater than vision. It is all combined. My brain becomes magnetized with this dominating force, which I hold in my hand— Bruce Lee.

What is your WHY?

It is the cause, purpose, or belief that drives you into a state of self-actualization. It defines the reason for your existence and why you get out of bed every morning. It is what sets you apart from everyone else and makes you unique. Those things inspire you and those around you to ACT, share in your ideas, or buy your product!

Not showing up is the number one reason most people fail. This is a very common and easy mistake to make.

Defining your why helps you gain a deeper understanding of yourself and influences everything you do. If you are an entrepreneur and don't know why you are in business or are not passionate about what you do, how would you convince clients to buy what you offer?

The whole point of defining your *why* is so that people can feel connected to what you offer – by building brand awareness and understanding. This way, you will stay focused and disciplined even through challenging times. Think of your *why* as the foundation of your success.

We all desire to live in a universal assignment—do what you are gifted or talented at, or able to do, and meet people's needs around you. This is what we should all aspire to be. However, finding your *why* is not a fixed point you must arrive and stay in. We live in a very dynamic world, and things change every day. Being motivated is not something you have, it is something you do, so what's in it for you? It is not enough to just be good at the task. You must want to do it and to push your skills.

Bill Gates, co-founder of Microsoft Corporation, author, investor, and Philanthropist, said that he had always wanted to work as a software developer. He did not foresee a time when he would leave his company to do anything else. Even with all his achievements, the self-made millionaire retired from Microsoft at the age of 40 to focus on the Gates Foundation geared toward helping solve health problems in developing countries.

What changed?

He found his purpose. He realized that his worldview was changing. The more he engages in solving health problems and touching lives across the world, the more he comes alive. In short, he dedicated himself to deep work by setting aside everything that distracted him so that he could focus obsessively on one task, philanthropy. When you are in deep work, the only thing that matters is the task at hand. It is this kind of obsessive attention that has allowed him to make real and impactful progress.

Cal Newport, author of Deep Work, said, "To learn hard things fast, we must be willing to focus intensely without letting in any distraction." In other words, learning is an act of deep work! If you shut out the world to just focus on the most important things, only then can you achieve enormous results.

Defining your *why* is like finding that point that keeps you focused on the target.

You must define your intentions and back them up with a focus and talent. We all can make a list of incredible goals we wish to achieve, but very few can check items off the list by giving something precious: attention! Achieving your goals is one thing but finding your true purpose that completes you is another.

Supposing you take a car apart into pieces, is it still a car? The car is not in its original state, which defines its function in life.

To find your why, you must clarify, understand, and communicate your purpose. Your purpose must be simple, clear, actionable, focused, and expressed in affirmative language that resonates with you. It should apply to everything you do professionally and personally.

But what is motivation?

I like to think of motivation as a process that helps one start and maintain a goal-oriented behavior. Motivation is not something you have, it is something you do. It pushes you to act. For you to be motivated, the biological, social, emotional, and cognitive forces must work together to activate the behavior, the driving force behind everything you do.

Perhaps you are wondering, *"But what lies behind the motivation? Why do we act in the first place?"*

According to Maslow's hierarchy of needs, we are motivated by the desire to fulfill our basic needs, like safety, psychological, esteem, social, and self-actualization. Our needs stir up internal pressure that influences our behavior.

- Safety needs are those that give a sense of security and well-being like a job with a secure salary
- Psychological needs are those that are necessary for our survival, like food, water, air, shelter, sleep, clothing, and medicine
- Social needs are those that offer us a sense of acceptance and belonging. They protect us from loneliness, isolation, and depression, like friendships, intimacy, and family
- Esteem needs are those that give us a sense of self-respect, which is more important than gaining others' respect and admiration, like promotions at the workplace
- Self-actualization needs are those that push us to break free from our comfort zones to reach our fullest potential

Motivation can either be intrinsic or extrinsic. Intrinsic motivation refers to the force that comes from within ourselves and for personal gratification—like doing a crossword puzzle. On the other hand, extrinsic motivation is reward driven and often involves rewards like public recognition and awards.

Think about one goal you have had in the past. Perhaps it was the desire to lose weight or run a marathon—was the desire enough? Desire is not enough to accomplish any goal. You must be willing to push through challenging situations and endure tough times to get through to the other side—achievement. In other words, for you to stay motivated, you must have three components:

- **Activation:** Actively deciding to initiate the behavior that will bring you closer to your goal

- **Willpower**: Continuously putting in effort to reach your goals no matter the challenges you face along the way. It is not about deprivation, but the ability to override thoughts, emotions and impulses telling you not to try. It is about delaying self-gratification in the short-term until you have achieved your goals. To have willpower, you must raise your self-awareness, meditate, exercise, eat well, and learn to relax. In essence, you are training the brain to pause before acting

- **Intensity**: This is the attention and vigor you need to pursue your goals

Realize that the extent of these components determines whether or not you reach your goals. When you have strong activation, there is a likelihood you will start chasing your goal. On the other hand, willpower and intensity will determine how much effort you are willing to put in to achieve your goals.

Perhaps you are thinking, *"How is purpose similar or different from motivation?"*

I like to think of purpose as an internal energy that boosts your motivation. There is no-one that can pressure you to have a purpose. If anyone tries to, they will only be depleting your motivation to act. Understand that purpose is not like the clothes you wear, it is not superficial. Instead, it is something that runs deep within you to create a path toward achieving something great.

Think back to the time when you felt most alive. You will realize that it is when you are more connected to others and energized by their ideas and general outlook of life. In that moment, you feel like you are not alone. You feel there is no pressure. You are naturally motivated to go after the things you want. You come alive when you gain mastery, wisdom and skill to get closer to your purpose—something greater than yourself.

The only way you can accept yourself fully is when you understand the things that motivate you. It allows you to uncover what makes you tick. Your motivation drives everything and connects you to your true self—not external factors like money, titles, and rewards.

So, how do you begin to write your story?

Reflection

Take a look within you; what story made you who you are? What story has shaped who you want to be in the world and how you impact others?

Finding your story is not that easy; even if it lies so close to you, it is hard to see it. While your story may feel like a series of events tangled together into a web to make you who you are, understanding every piece of the puzzle goes a long way in shaping the story.

Imagine a light focused through a magnifying glass. Its power can burn a piece of paper. If you focus it even more, like a laser beam, it can cut through steel. Just like light focused through a magnifying glass, having a clear sense of purpose allows you to focus your efforts on the things that truly matter. It will compel you to take risks and push through all obstacles.

Unlike animals, we are driven by way more than mere survival. Without our *WHY*, we easily get distracted, disillusioned, and give up. It is the reason many people resort to drug use, suicidal behaviors, and depression. Knowing your purpose helps you figure out how to achieve goals that excite you. Defining your *WHY* will compel you to focus your attention on actions that will propel you into a new, more challenging, and rewarding trajectory.

In other words, if your goals are infused with a sense of *WHY*, you will not feel like you are struggling but instead becoming what you are meant to be in the first place–more of yourself. Think of your WHY as an eternal condition of success. If you find yourself trying to pay attention to simple tasks with no success, it helps to imbue them with a purpose to make them easier to accomplish. With a purpose, attention comes naturally.

Today, I want you to ask yourself, "Can I create purpose around everything I do?" Infusing even the most mundane tasks with purpose will make a difference. Talk to your friends, family, and those close to you to find out what they see lights you up. Those that are closest to us can see us more clearly than we see ourselves.

Adopt a positive mindset

Watch your thoughts, they become your words; watch your words, they become your actions; watch your actions, they become your habits; watch your habits, they become your character; watch your character, it becomes your destiny

—Lao Tzu.

Perhaps you are wondering, *"What is positive thinking?"*

Well, this is a mental and emotional attitude that concentrates on the good and expects beneficial results. It revolves around anticipating health, happiness, and success. The way you think about yourself can make or break you. What you think affects your actions, which in turn determines whether or not you achieve success in what you do. It influences your worldview and the quality of your relationships.

I hear people say things like, "I can't do it. I don't have what it takes to succeed. I don't like it."

That is negativity at work! When you allow negativity to come in, you talk yourself out of your goals. You give away your willpower, motivation, and efficiency.

The most important thing is that you change the blueprint and all it takes is for you to decide!

To control your life and purpose, you must decide to start each day with positive energy. Set smart goals, pursue them, manage change, achieve success, and celebrate every win, whether big or small, to help you replicate and manifest more success. The only way you will adopt positivity is when you realize that it is all up to you. When you decide to take charge of your emotions, you can direct your mindset in the right direction despite all outside influences.

Taking charge of your thoughts, actions, and feelings allows everything in your life to fall into place. Yes, you may not control every event that happens in your life, but you can control your response. When you empower yourself to change what is within your control, you can release your brakes and allow yourself to break through the horizons to experience growth you never imagined before.

Key Takeaway Points

- Your *WHY* is the cause, purpose, or belief that drives you into a state of self-actualization
- Being motivated is not something you have, it is something you do
- You must define your intentions and back them up with a focus and talent
- Your purpose must be simple, clear, actionable, focused, and expressed in affirmative language that resonates with you

- To control your life and purpose, you must decide to start each day with positive energy
- Taking charge of your thoughts, actions, and feelings allows everything in your life to fall into place

Chapter 6 Focus

Clear Vision

2020 was a year that meant different things for different people. It was the 21st day of lockdown, and I felt like my whole life had come to a standstill. I looked out through the window and what struck me was the beauty of the Universe: the trees, birds, clouds in the sky, and buildings. No one was out in the streets. For the first time in my life, I asked myself, "Why am I here?" "Why are all these things here, including the coronavirus?"

My mind was racing so fast, trying to find an answer to every question that popped up. These are the questions that humanity has been trying to answer for most of its existence and yet, no answer we come up with seems to point at one thing that explains the whole essence of our existence. I asked myself, "Will I find out the reason for my existence when I die, and if so, what is the point?" If heaven and hell exist, what good will the punishment or reward do if we can't remember our past life and its lessons or even the crimes we are being punished for? Is it possible that all the beauty and ugliness we see in the world today has a reason for their existence?

As I pondered over these questions, a thought came to mind: "*Hope!*" I knew that things would not be this way forever. I realized that I still had so many dreams and desires waiting to be fulfilled. As I sipped my cup of green tea, I started designing my vision board, what I wanted in life and how I would achieve it.

Yes, the present did not make sense to me, but I did not allow that to stand in the way of my future. I saw hope—my dreams and desires coming to reality—and chose to focus on that!

I like what the Bible says in Proverbs 29:18: "Without a vision, my people perish."

Perhaps you feel like you are trying to find your way on a misty path. You don't have a clear vision of where you want to be, what you want in life, or how to get there. It feels like you are going around in circles every single day only to find yourself in the same spot you started. You feel lost, but you are not alone. We all feel like we don't know where we are going at some point in life.

I will let you in on a secret. Focus is not something you have, it is something you do.

But what does focus mean in the first place?

Focus is your center of interest. If you want to concentrate on one thing, you must ignore other things. In other words, one thing–the most important and valuable one–must take your center of interest. You can only focus when you have said yes to one thing and no to all others. You must eliminate to focus. I like what Tim Ferris, author of *9 Habits to Stop Now*, once said: "What you don't do determines what you can do."

The Law of Concentration states that what you persistently and consciously put your mind to, will grow. In short, the more you reflect on something, the more it will impact your behavior, choices, and actions.

Your focus is key to creating mindful intentions, which goes a long way in helping you manifest everything you want–and remember, creating anything takes effort. Understand that your mind is your creator and can also be a distractor. If you don't take control of your mind and direct it to focus on your goals, there is a high likelihood nothing will get done. By getting rid of distractions, you are choosing to stay on track. When you focus on your thoughts, you give them life.

You don't need to say no to tasks permanently. Instead, you need to say a present NO! There is always an option to do something else later. In the present moment, you must draw your attention to one thing. By saying NO to all else, you get a chance to unlock your ability to complete the one most important and valuable task left!

Even amid all challenges and life's distractions, you must choose to focus on the most important things in life. If you choose to focus on important aspects of your life, they will expand. If you choose to focus on distractions and challenges, they too will expand. If you want to change something in your life—habits, career, family—your focus should not be on fighting the old. Instead, it should be on building the new. In other words, life will change if you decide to take responsibility for changing it.

Today, I want you to start working to change. That is how your life will get better. The Pareto Principle, also called the 80/20 Rule, suggests that 20% of what you do will account for at least 80% of your outcomes. In other words, if you have ten items on your to-do list, two of them will turn out to be worth more than the other eight combined.

Unfortunately, most people habitually procrastinate on the most important and valuable items and spend their energy focusing 80% on trivial tasks that will not contribute significant results. To effectively apply this principle, you must start by setting goals. Here's how you do it:

- Take a piece of paper and list ten goals you want to achieve
- Ask yourself, "What is the one goal I would choose to accomplish on this list that has the greatest positive impact on my life?"
- Repeat the same to identify the second most important goal

You will have identified 20% of goals that are worth your focus and energy and that will prove more valuable in your life than anything. If you take the time to understand this principle, you will realize its importance in prioritizing tasks and the time you have every day.

> *What I hear I forget*
> *What I see I remember*
> *What I do I understand*
>
> -Chinese Proverb.

The starting point for great success has always been the same: daring to dream big!

Cast off your limitations and channel your energy on your biggest dreams. Here's the key to living a limitless life:

- **Clarity:** You must be clear about who you are, what you want, and where you are headed. With this kind of clarity, your focus every day will be on your goals

- **Competence**: You must become very good at what you do. Applying the 80/20 rule in everything you do will ensure that you dedicate your focus and energy to the most valuable and important tasks—

those that will elevate you to greater heights of success. When you do this, you continuously learn that excellence is a moving target, and you must keep growing to reach your goals

- **Concentration**: You must possess the self-discipline to pay attention to one thing at a time—the most important thing—until completion. In other words, success is the sum of focus and concentration

That said, the focus is about knowing precisely what you want to be, what you have, and need to do to become. Today, allow yourself to look through the window and overlook all the distractions that lie before you so that you can dream big. Be intentional in using your attention and time and choose to focus your energy on overcoming your major constraints. When you do this, you will feel immense power and confidence flowing through you to the things you love to do and realize your full potential.

How to focus to activate your attention

If you ask anyone, they will tell you that they wish they could be more focused. Attention has quickly become an untamable beast in a busy world full of distractions. According to Milstein et al., (2005), people who can sustain attention for extended durations regularly perform better in all kinds of cognitive challenges. However, when you are easily distracted, the chances are that you are poor at decision-making and your creativity level is low.

Is our problem that we get distracted?

Unfortunately, most people don't practice how to stay focused. The brain is a muscle, and that means you can build it. When you take a more realistic approach to build your focus, you will be amazed at all the things you can do that you thought you couldn't. To build your attention and learn the art of focusing, you must first understand the power of focus and then establish the right environment, habits, and mindsets you wish to promote.

What is your reason for wanting to build your ability to focus? For most people, these reasons vary from wanting improved productivity, learning new skills, building a superior product, gaining success, or just trying to protect themselves from distractions at the workplace. Whatever your reasons, learning how to focus will help you get more done in less time. In other words, if you can master how to tap into the power of your focus, only then can you be productive.

Remember, we all have 24 hours in a day. The most important thing is not how you use that time but the intensity of your focus. If you increase your attention's intensity, you can get a lot done in a minimal time. Irrespective of whether you are in a state of flow, attention can help you make the most of your day.

According to a study conducted by Mark et al., (2008) at the University of California, an average person can work on a project for 11 minutes before being distracted. Interestingly, once one is distracted, it takes at least 25 minutes to regain attention.

If you learn how to stay focused, you know how to be productive. Focus determines whether you do what you want to do or spend the entire day distracted. It is not about being better at work. It is the foundation of all your life experiences. It helps you choose the life you want to live without reacting to the events happening around you.

One of my favorite methods for focusing on what matters is by getting rid of what doesn't. This is Warren Buffet's 2-list strategy. So, how does it work?

Buffet first asked his pilot, Mike Flint, to list his top 25 goals, which he did. Buffet then asked Flint to circle his top five goals, and he did. At this point, Flint had two lists: five items circled and 20 non-circled. Flint said that he was going to get started on the five goals immediately. "But what of the list of items you did not circle?" asked Buffet. Flint responded that the first five were his primary goals while the other 20 were secondary and he would work on them intermittently as he saw fit.

What would you do?

The things you don't circle are the ones you avoid at all costs. They are the things that don't get your attention no matter what until you achieve your top five goals. When it comes to your attention, you need to learn to make tough decisions and eliminate the things that waste your focus. The tasks that derail your focus are those you easily justify working on. Using this method will help you eliminate distractions and narrow your focus on what matters the most.

That said, your attention will begin to fade after a period of time irrespective of what method you choose or how committed you are. So, how can you increase your attention span and stay focused?

One of the best ways is using the Loci technique. The term *loci* mean location. This method is based on attaching items you wish to recall to specific points along a familiar path—room, route to work, college, etc. This way, you can remember them as you walk along the path in your mind. For instance, to boost your focus and memory visualization of a project you have been working on, you can create a path for it, like your path from your parking lot to the bedroom. When you come out of the car, you walk up the stairs to the entryway. The front door opens to the living room, the dining area, and leads to the kitchen. Down the hallway, you walk past your home office and the guest cloakroom before ending up in the bedroom.

The trick is, you can take each of these points: parking, stairway, front entry, living room, dining room, kitchen, hallway, office, cloakroom, and bedroom, and assign them to the different components of your project. Building an association between your project and a familiar path does not only help you remember but focuses your attention on even the smallest details.

Measure results

The first thing you need to do is measure progress. Anthony Robbins, American author, coach, speaker, and philanthropist, acknowledges that "progress equals happiness." It is the steps of achievement and growth that give us the greatest satisfaction. The reason your attention is fading is because of a lack of feedback. The human brain is wired to want to know how its performing. How far is it from achieving the main goal? It is impossible to measure progress when there is no feedback. Therefore, you must measure your results.

Are there areas you consider important to you? Have you measured your progress lately? If not, then that might explain why your attention has been fading away. You must understand that what you measure is what you can improve. When you have the numbers, you can track whether you are getting better or worse.

For instance, if you are trying to get fit by walking every day, measuring how many steps you make will help you get stronger at the end of the day. When you track your reading habits for several pages by the end of the day, only then can you read more books. The moment you record your values, you start living intentionally and with integrity.

In short, the tasks you measure are the ones you attend to.

But why do we avoid measuring in the first place?

The fear of what numbers will reveal to us is fear of failure. You must realize that measuring tasks does not say much about who you are but gives you feedback on where you are. Always measure your progress to discover what you did not know and gain deeper insight. This gives you an opportunity to reset your compass, analyze what you need to do differently to get back on the right track. Rather than measuring how much time you spend on a task, focus on your progress toward knowing yourself better. This will help you pay attention to the things that matter most and ignore those that don't.

Pay attention to the process rather than the event

The next thing you can do to increase your attention span is to put your mind on the process and not the event. How many times have you considered the completion of project success? How many times have you told yourself, if I can just lose 10 pounds (4.5 kilograms), I will get back in shape? If I just get my manuscript published, then I will earn credibility.

Your health, career, or business are not events. The moment you pay attention to your goals, you realize that none of these things are events. It is your commitment to the process that makes the real difference. It is what makes you fall in love with the daily activities that steer you towards achieving your goals. Concentrating your attention on the process allows you to enjoy the results.

Yes, you might want to be a great writer and become the next bestseller, and that is great. But to reach that goal, you must fall in love with the writing process. Or perhaps you want your business to be known worldwide and be featured in *The Wall Street* Journal. However, you must fall in love with marketing your business to the world. Generally, to get better at anything, you must fall in love with the process of doing it. Fall in love with the business of building your identity of someone doing the work and not just dreaming of the results.

Don't get me wrong; there is nothing wrong when you focus on goals and results. However, paying attention to the process will earn you consistent results in the long term.

Doing the right activities will get you the right results!

To get started, here's what you need to do:

Select an anchor task

What is that one task you must do without any negotiations? Make this the mainstay that holds the rest of your day in place. Remember what we said about multitasking–it doesn't work! Even though you plan to get many things done, one task you prioritize is your anchor task. When you choose a priority task every day, it helps guide your behavior throughout the day by organizing your routine around that one task.

Manage your attention, not time

Identify the task that calls for your undivided attention, and then schedule it for when you are beaming with energy. We are all different. I consider the afternoon when my creative energy is high. This is when my mind is fresh, not distracted and is the best time to write. Afternoons are when I make strategic decisions about every aspect of my life—family, business, and career. Other tasks like meetings, crunching on numbers, phone calls, and emailing come in the morning.

Attention revolves around eliminating distractions. If you ask most people, the common denominator is emailing. If you spend your creative energy reading and responding to emails, what happens when that energy dissipates? I like what Brian Tracy, Canadian-American motivational public speaker and self-development author of a popular book, *Earn What You're Worth, Eat That Frog!* once said: "*If you have to eat two frogs, eat the ugliest one first.*" In other words, start with the most critical task always, one that moves you toward your goals. When you do this, no matter what comes your way during the day, you have done what's most important! You don't sit and allow the rest of the world to dictate your mental state and where your energy goes.

Does it mean attention management will eliminate all distractions for your day?

Definitely not!

However, it will raise your awareness of these distractions. This way, you will build your attention muscle, reclaim back the control of your attention, and commit yourself to the things that matter most.

Remember, each time you are distracted, all you need to do is refocus your attention on what matters most. It may be challenging at first, but once you get the hang of it, you will be grateful you chose what deserved your attention. The most important thing is you get started!

Make music

We don't need science to know that music plays a key role in boosting brain power and getting you in a good mood. Have you ever wondered why doctors listen to music while they operate – especially in medical dramas? Because music motivates, improves mood, eliminates distractions, and helps the mind focus on the task at hand. The key is to choose the right music for the right task.

Even with all of the brain's amazing abilities, it has not evolved to process abstract information or spend a long time pondering over one thing. We tend to have the conscious attention that directs our focus toward the things that matter, and the unconscious one tends to shift attention around things, possibly significant things our senses pick. This unconscious attention system is linked to our emotional processes rather than higher reasoning. It acts fast such that when you hear some noise while you are home alone, you pay attention to it in an attempt to figure out what it might be and where it is coming from.

Unfortunately, even when conscious attention is focused on what you are doing, the unconscious attention system does not power off. It is busy scanning for anything in the background. If what you are doing is not exciting, the unconscious attention system becomes more potent. In other words, a distraction does not necessarily have to be stimulating to steal your attention.

How many times has an office mate annoyed you with the most innocuous thing like sipping coffee, tapping a pen on the desk, or singing aloud when you are trying to work on an important task? Is it them or the task you are paying attention to? The chances are what you are doing is not stimulating for the brain and this where music comes in handy. It effectively neutralizes the unconscious attention system and puts you in a good mood to concentrate on the most important task.

Think of music as a small toy you give a child to play with while you have a conversation with a guest or get some work done. However, just because it is music does not mean it will increase your concentration in every task. Different kinds of music match different tasks. If you need attention to write a new article, you need full attention, unlike when clearing your inbox and organizing your desktop.

Suppose you are engaging in a language-heavy task like writing, reading, or taking a test. Listening to loud music can be distracting. The wrong type of music for the right task can render you less efficient. If you are doing important tasks that call for your undivided attention, go for nature sounds—like flowing water, animal noises, bird calls—and classical music, which sharpen your attention and ease the mind. These kinds of music stimulate feelings of positivity.

If you are working out, like running or weightlifting at the gym, go for high-energy music like rap, rock, or pop songs. These kinds of music will boost your physical performance, improving your motivation and strength.

Listening to your favorite music is a good way to trigger the release of feel-good hormones, which lowers stress levels and feelings of anxiety. What better way to help your mind pay attention than the music you love? Always get the most out of your attention by matching tunes to tasks. Once you get it right, music will be your new workmate, helping your mind achieve clarity, focus, and insight.

How to adjust your thinking to activate your attention

Mindfulness ego vs. aligned self

It is early morning and still dark. I wake up and hear gentle pitter-patter on my tin roof. I get up, open the curtain and look out of the window. It's raining. Good. I don't have to train! My mind starts sabotaging my ability to justify the thought: I'm not good enough ... I'm not as fast as I need to be ... I'm never going to make it anyway ... I feel like I am an impostor ... I'm worried that I will injure myself ... Overthinking with negative thoughts, I stop and consider what I am doing and why I am thinking this way. Quickly, I recognize that I am in a surviving ego mode that harms my progress. Intentionally, I try to change my mindset with positive, decisive thoughts. I am open to try ... I am authentic and I have faith that with practice I can do this ... I need patience and trust ... I am going to get changed now and go for a run ... That is my attention and focus for now ... I will feel better for it.

We tend to talk ourselves out of our goals and dreams, postpone, or allow fear to get in the way. What we are doing is building a self-belief against what we wish to achieve. This belief takes the driver's seat of our lives. It's the easy way out. It's like we have given up control of our lives, and we are just spiraling. Over the years, we have picked up baggage and set roadblocks for our lives. The most common one is ego, the person we have become to like and accept us. It is the person we convince ourselves that we are without question. It is the person others have made us believe that we are.

What would it be like if we got rid of this ego? What if you employed mindfulness ego–restructuring the emotional impact of our ego–instead? What if you let go of all the baggage you have picked up over the years?

You want to get free from the tyranny of your ego-mind. The whole point is to unhook yourself and your identity from what others have made you believe that you are. The secret of mindful ego is to help you see everything happening inside without ownership or judgment. When you allow others to define who you are, your attention shifts from your true self, and your minds drag you around, forcing you to interact with each thought and feeling you and others generate.

You don't need to respond to everything the mind generates. You get to choose where to place your attention and how to live your life. You don't need to be the mind. Instead, you can use your mind to raise your awareness of every thought and feeling without responding. In other words, adopting a mindful ego ensures that you come first in that moment of solitude and still afford others your undivided attention when in their company. This is how you align yourself with who you truly are inside.

This is one of the ideologies of Mia Hewett, founder of Aligned Intelligence ™ and author of *Meant for More*. I like what Mia Hewett said: "Being a force to be reckoned with by learning what it takes to have what you think, what you say, how you feel, and what you do all in alignment. This is Power."

I have been using this strategy successfully over the past few years. Being conscious of my unconscious sabotaging. Quickly turning negative unconstructive thoughts into positive, empowering thoughts. And, being present in the moment, controlling my attention, focusing on my activities to achieve my goals.

I hope that today, you will look beyond your limitations and everyday struggles to your biggest dreams. I pray that you realize that you are enough and meant for more, and you will stretch your focus to the things that will help you reach your full potential. Don't allow anything to hold you back. Struggling is not fun. Let go of everything standing in the way of your greatness and embrace what the future holds in store for you.

It is simple—all you have to do is FOCUS!

Key Takeaway Points

- Focus simply is your center of interest
- Saying NO to all else offers you a chance to unlock your ability to complete the one most important and valuable task left
- Energy flows where your attention goes. Be intentional in using your attention and time, and choose to focus your energy on overcoming your major constraints

- Life will change if you decide to take responsibility for changing it
- The Pareto Principle, also called the 80/20 Rule, suggests that 20% of what you do will account for at least 80% of your outcomes
- Cast off your limitations and channel your energy on your biggest dreams
- The keys to living a limitless life:
    - *Clarity*
    - *Competence*
    - *Concentration*
- To increase your attention span and stay focused, you must:
    - Measure results
    - Pay attention to the process rather than the event by
        - *Selecting an anchor task*
        - *Managing your attention, not time*
- Listening to your favorite music is a good way to trigger the release of feel-good hormones, which lowers stress levels and feelings of anxiety
- You don't need to respond to everything the mind generates. You get to choose where to place your attention and how to live your life

- Adopting a mindful ego ensures that you come first in that moment of solitude and still afford others your undivided attention when in their company

Your mind will always believe everything you tell it.
Feed it hope.
Feed it truth.
Feed it with love

—Stardust Poetry.

Chapter 7 Flow

Going With the Flow

Empty your mind; be formless, shapeless – like water. Now you put water into a cup; it becomes the cup, you put water into a bottle, it becomes the bottle, you put it in a teapot, it becomes the teapot. Now water can flow, or it can crash. Be water, my friend.

–Bruce Lee.

I read a Taoist story of a man that accidentally fell over a cliff into a river. The water was flowing so fast to a dangerous waterfall that had killed many people in the past. There were many onlookers at the scene of events who feared for the man's life. To cut a long story short, the man miraculously came out alive downstream.

Everyone was full of questions, "How did he survive?"

This is what the old man responded, "I accommodated myself to the water, not the water to me. Without thinking, I allowed myself to be shaped by it. Plunging into the swirl, I came out with the swirl. This is how I survived."

What would you do if you were this man?

Perhaps you would try to control the situation by fighting with the water flow to get back upstream. Most of us do when faced with challenging situations—control things because they are not going according to plan. When you don't know where the path leads, you get frustrated. When you find out that the meeting was canceled without your knowledge, you want to try and get things, like everything else, in order.

We have heard people tell us to go with the flow of events and energy.

The Law of Flow states that everything is energy, the ability to do work. Your energy flows where your attention goes. In that case, the state of anything depends on the frequency at which the energy is vibrating. Assuming that something is static, in that case, its energy level is low. However, when energy is flowing at an acceptable level, it is effective in all regions. If it flows at full speed, there is a chance creativity, damage, and destruction will happen.

But, what if the outflow energy matches the inflow energy? What happens then?

In that state, the flow of energy is most productive, effective, and successful. At that level, there is no strain, drain, or leakage. In other words, the flow of energy is happening at the correct level. When energy does not flow at the correct level, blockages and destructions are likely to happen. However, when you balance the flow of energy, you achieve optimal performance which applies to everything meaningful in your life.

But what does it mean to go with the flow?

It simply means responding to changes and disruptions calmly and creatively. Even when faced with a challenging situation, you must stay level-headed, flexible, and adaptive to get through it. You must be willing to shift your priorities without necessarily abandoning your goals. Like the old man, you must not try to fight the situation. Instead, master a special kind of creativity to make room for fresh opportunities to emerge.

Flow is the mental state in which you fully immerse yourself in tasks with an energized focus, known colloquially as being "in the zone." In other words, you are fully absorbed in something that the outer world does not seem to exist. It happens when you decide to follow your heart.

When you are in a state of flow, your ego falls away, and you don't even notice time flying. Just like playing a musical instrument, your actions, movements, and thoughts flow seamlessly. Your entire being is involved in the process, and you realize that your skills are optimally used. While flow happens differently for different people, it often happens when you immerse yourself in something you are passionate and skilled in.

Don't get me wrong, I am not saying that you should control or relinquish your responsibilities. Going with the flow is about choosing to concentrate on things that truly matter, spending little time trying to control events, being open to new and exciting opportunities, and letting go of all unnecessary pressure from within or without.

Yes, there are times when the ebb and flow may not be appropriate like when you receive sudden news that calls for immediate attention. However, you can allow yourself to stay in the moment with your attention zeroed in on the most important thing.

Take a moment to imagine yourself soaking in the serenity of nature. You can see and hear the river flow, birds singing, trees swaying from side to side, and a beautiful breeze kissing your skin. There is no resistance. Nature simply allows itself to be transformed by the flow.

Flow moves in the right direction. You don't have to put in the effort to get things where they are supposed to be. Tapping into the power of the flow is allowing yourself to live in harmony with nature. Instead of controlling everything happening around you, flow draws your attention to what is right in front of you. You don't have to chase it. All you need to do is breathe and release. Instead of trying to swim upstream, why not let the water carry you where it flows?

The reason we experience difficulties is because our focus is in the wrong place—self-judgment. We think that going up is good and doing down is bad. We think that happiness is right and pain is wrong. We fail to realize that all these emotions are essential and necessary for our learning and growth.

Imagine a bamboo plant; how many nodules does it have? Many! Does that mean it is a bad thing? It is the nodules that give it strength. They are not meant to damage it but give it strength. The same goes for our lives; when we face difficulties and challenges, it is an opportunity for us to grow. We should direct our attention to finding the lesson rather than the hurt.

It is simple—acceptance brings flow. Staying in the present moment is choosing to draw power from the reality of what is and not what we would have it. When you are conscious of what is happening, you allow your focus to shift toward growth rather than being consumed by events.

Be like a tree; let the dead leaves drop

–Rumi.

How to get in a state of flow to activate your attention

When was the last time you were fully immersed in a task only to realize that time had melted away?

The good thing is that you don't have to sit around waiting for the flow to happen. You can act and access it. I love flow because it guides everything meaningful in your life—relationships, career, and even passions. Flow is something that happens to us and not just for the athletes, creatives, or academicians. It is the optimal state of mind where you feel and perform your best.

Experiencing flow is the ultimate goal. The state where everything you do is effortless and enjoyable. The key elements of flow include:

- Extreme attention on tasks
- Active control
- Merged actions and awareness
- Distorted experience of time

In a state of flow, you create a euphoric experience that keeps you coming back for more. In that state, the brain triggers the release of neurochemicals like:

- **Norepinephrine**: Tightens your focus on the task at hand by shutting out all the persistent multitasking distractions

- **Endorphins:** Blocks pain and allows you to burn the candle at both ends without burning out

- **Anandamide:** Promotes lateral neural connections that trigger more insight than any brainstorming session would ever do

- **Serotonin:** Is a feel-good hormone that allows you to gel with your team more powerfully and intentionally

In short, the state of flow triggers the brain to work on overdrive, allowing you to process complex information smoothly and helps you think deeply without even realizing it.

That said, how do you get into that state of flow?

There is no one-size-fits-all technique. This is because we are different, and hence experience flows differently. What triggers flow for one is not the same for another. You must be willing to act and invite flow into everything you focus on.

Step 1 Identify your natural state of flow

Just like most, you have experienced a state of flow without realizing it. Think back to when you were completely immersed in something that you completely lost track of time. What is it that you were doing when hours passed by without realizing it? Was it something you loved doing, like painting, writing, crafting, sport, gamification, or something else? What was it?

The other indicator of flow is when you feel that things just gel in together. Perhaps it was a time when you realized you had new ideas and insights that came together in ways you had never done it before.

Flow is a feature of a positive feedback loop. In other words, the more you immerse yourself in a task, the more positive feedback you get, and the more motivated you are to keep doing it. While flow happens in a passive state—when you are watching TV, reading, writing, or playing—the actual state of flow happens in an active state.

Step 2 Work backward

Now that you know when you last experienced flow, the next step is to determine how to get there. The trick here is to recreate memories of when you experienced flow and then examine them. The first thing is to observe yourself for a length of time, say two or three weeks. Take note of what you do and record any key indicators of flow, like losing track of time, acting effortlessly, gaining new ideas and insight, and having a positive feedback loop.

Once you get into that state of flow, you must work on widening your awareness. Take note of everything happening around you. What is it that you are doing physically when you lose track of time or feel like everything is effortless? Also, take note of what is happening in your mind.

I realized that my state of flow comes when I am running or playing soccer. Physically, I am outside working out. However, my inner emotions run deeper because I want to support my soccer team and create synergy among them that generates a sense of belonging. My state of flow is not just when I am running or kicking a ball but also when I am taking part in a group dynamic.

When I tap into my state of flow, everything happens effortlessly: communication, working, and conversations.

Step 3 Understand the benefits of flow

This plays a key role in helping us reinforce the habit. Understand that the more you experience a flow, the more you will look for opportunities to enjoy the rewards. Unfortunately, people get into a state of flow every day only to shut it down because they think it's not practical or unrealistic. However, if a state of flow aligns you to your best self, you have a better chance of experiencing satisfaction, fulfillment, problem-solving, and influence. Who wouldn't want that?

Step 4 Shift into your flow state purposefully

You don't have to wait for flow to strike. Instead, you must ease yourself into the flow and make it a routine, just like taking out the trash, taking a shower, or brushing your teeth. The more you practice, the easier it gets to just snap into the flow. Take note of all the physical and emotional steps you take that lead up to flow. Record where you are, what you are doing, and how you feel, and then repeat them.

I have mentioned earlier that we experience flow differently. Perhaps you are good at solving mathematical problems or when giving feedback. Making flow accessible and repeatable helps set the stage for your best self to show up often, and the best part is that you get to pass the same benefits to others because the flow is contagious!

When I reflect, I can see that my mind is fixed on what is the now, watching what is going on around me, listening to the beat of music or instructions, feeling the vibe, anticipating and reacting to challenges, and tasting a win. My actions and mindfulness are unified.

Step 5 Do pre-flow training

To harness your focus, meditation and mindfulness play a key role. To get into a state of flow, spending five minutes on mindfulness meditation and focusing on your breathing can be rewarding. Start by finding a comfortable place to sit: the floor, chair, or anywhere you feel relaxed. Close your eyes and note every sensation on your body—where the body touches the chair and how it feels. Are there parts of the body where you feel weighty or light, even or uneven? Let go of any tension you feel on your muscles. Let your shoulders drop, lower your chin, and ensure your spine is upright.

Inhale for four counts, hold it for three counts, and then exhale for five counts. Notice your breathing, and don't try to change or force it. Take note of the air flowing through your nostrils, traveling down the lungs, into the abdomen, and fading away. If you notice your mind begin to wander, follow it where it goes and gently pull it back to the center of your attention—breathing. Don't allow your thoughts to frustrate you. Just notice your thoughts come and go without judgment. The trick is to train your mind to stay in the present.

Step 6 Get rid of any distractions and quit multitasking

When we say getting rid of distractions, it also includes physically removing them. Whenever you find yourself falling victim to task-switching, gently remove the distraction—like switching off your phone, clearing your desk, closing all tabs on the laptop, turning off notifications, and then getting work done.

Take a minute to reflect on all your tasks. You will notice that most of those that take away your attention are mindless: receiving a call, chatting with friends, gossiping, reading a blog post, watching Tik-Tok, or scrolling through social media. If we are honest, these are shallow tasks that are not worth our attention and focus. While you may feel productive performing them, they are distractions that get in the way of your flow.

Remember, your brain is designed to vibrate at the same level as your task at hand, one at a time. When distracted by this and that, the brain strains, and you begin to drift from your state of flow. To remain in a state of flow, make tasks mean something to you. Everything you do does not necessarily have to be your life's true calling. However, you must attach meaning to everything you do. You can do this by setting goals and giving immediate positive feedback, which balances the inflow and outflow of energy flow.

Step 7 Challenge yourself enough

The only way you can be engaged in a task is when you are at its sweet spot of completing it while feeling challenged by its complexity. If something you are doing is not challenging enough, you will likely get distracted or bored. It pulls you out of the flow state. On the other hand, if a task is way too complex, you will likely freeze or get frustrated by it. It is one thing to challenge yourself to think outside the box, and it is another to overstretch beyond your capabilities. Overstretching puts you out of the flow. You no longer vibrate at the same energy as your task.

But what if you engage in tasks that are just challenging, ones that stretch you just enough?

In that case, you get to the sweet spot where the flow is optimal, and your attention is grounded on the task at hand. There is a rule that you should engage in tasks that are approximately 4% more difficult than your perceived ability. Anything above 4% complexity throws you off balance, and you miss the flow channel.

That said, you have to challenge yourself just enough and then take breaks in between. Being in flow can be incredibly taxing for the brain and your energy levels. It is not possible to stay in flow throughout the day; you will burn out every day. The trick here is to take short breaks between flow attempts to stretch, hit the reset button, and reenergize. This way, you can easily repeat the cycle of flow, focus your attention, and become productive.

Key Takeaway Points

- Flow is the mental state in which a person performing some activity is fully immersed in a feeling of energized focus–being in the *ZONE*
- Flow is not something you have, it is something you do
- Everything is energy
- When energy does not flow at the correct level, blockages and destructions are likely to happen

- When you are in a state of flow, your ego falls away, and you don't even notice time flying
- The reason we see experience difficulties is because our focus is in the wrong place, and we self-judge
- The key elements of flow include:
    - Extreme attention on tasks
    - Active control
    - Merged actions and awareness
    - Distorted experience of time
- What triggers flow for one is not the same for another. You must be willing to act and invite flow into everything you focus on by:
    - Step 1 Identify your natural state of flow
    - Step 2 Work backward
    - Step 3 Understand the benefits of flow
    - Step 4 Shift into your flow state purposefully
    - Step 5 Do pre-flow training
    - Step 6 Get rid of any distractions and quit multitasking
    - Step 7 Challenge yourself enough

Time is like a river.
You cannot touch the same water twice, because the flow that has passed will never pass again.
Enjoy every moment of your life!

—www.livelifehappy.com

Chapter 8 Procrastination

Should I, or Shouldn't I?

Tomorrow is a day that never comes, at least for a procrastinator. I read a story by Arnold Lobel, author of the book *Days with Frog and Toad*. One day, the toad woke up to a messy house. He said to himself, "I have so much work to do." On looking through the window at the mess, the frog agreed with the toad.

You would think that the toad would go ahead and clean up the mess, right?

Instead, he went back to bed and said, "I will do it tomorrow. Today, I will take it easy." The frog came into the house and tried alerting the Toad to all the work waiting for him, but Toad said he would do it "tomorrow." "I will clean the dishes, dust the chair, scrub the windows, water the plants, etc. ... tomorrow!"

The next day, the toad woke up, sat on the edge of the bed, thinking of all the things he would do *tomorrow*. Frog told him, "Tomorrow will be hard for you. But if you clean up today, you will not have to do it tomorrow."

How many things have you allocated to tomorrow? Has tomorrow yet arrived? How long will tomorrow take? How many piles of work are waiting for tomorrow? Have you thought about how that would work out for you? What if you did those tasks today?

Tomorrow, tomorrow, tomorrow–it never comes!

Procrastination is the act of putting off tasks to a later time. This little tactic creates conflicts between the mind and the body. It resides in the gray area between self-care and motivation. It happens when you are not sure what choice to make–should I, or should I not? The funny part is that most people fall into the trap of quitting too soon just so that they can do it later. You don't know that when you procrastinate, you are choosing to overwork later to the point of diminishing returns.

Procrastination is not something you have, it is something you do. The law of the Universe believes there is a lot about our lives we absolutely cannot control. However, you can control how you respond because it is in your response that your greatest power lies. The only way to defeat procrastination is to know yourself and balance your motivation with your attention.

Perhaps you are thinking, *"There are times when your mind says yes, but the body says no. What should I do? Should I force myself through the task regardless of quality? Is it all right to do a shoddy job just because you are exhausted?"*

Pushing yourself too hard when you can't focus will only lower your productivity. Forcing yourself to work when your energy levels are low will not benefit you. Think about it—it's Tuesday, and you have a headache. You decide to push yourself, get one task done before heading home. What happens? You complete the task, but the week's stamina is gone! On Wednesday, Thursday, and Friday, you complete fewer tasks than usual and push the remainder to the next week.

This means, when you pushed yourself on Tuesday, you got one task done, but five tasks pushed to the coming week.

But what if you accepted your energy levels and went home on Tuesday? You would be well rested and come the following day reenergized and ready to get things done.

This is not always the case. Sometimes it is 3.00 p.m., and you have a report to complete. Should you complete it or not?

Yes, procrastination is not all black and white, but pushing yourself beyond your capability will not help you achieve optimal productivity. However, the most potent tool you have is attention. You can have all the time and money, but you will not get any work done without attention.

Why do you Procrastinate?

Most people think they procrastinate because they are lazy, unorganized, or stressed out–but that is not the case. The reason you procrastinate is that you cannot regulate your emotions. John Ferrari, a psychology professor and author of *Still Procrastinating: The No-Regrets Guide to Getting It,* said telling a procrastinator just to do it is like telling someone with depression to cheer up!

Procrastination has nothing to do with time management, just like it has nothing to do with willpower. Whenever you are faced with a decision or a task, you rely on your self-control to push yourself to get it done. We tend to get things done when we expect to get a reward for our efforts.

You do it because you cannot self-regulate your mood and emotions around the tasks at hand. In most cases, you know exactly what you need to do, but you cannot bring yourself to do it. The gap between attention and action is huge. If you ask yourself why you are procrastinating, you will likely write a long list of all the reasons why something you wanted to do never happened. The thing is, you cannot get results if you don't act. The problem is that by projecting our worries and fears out into the future, that we stop acting. We allow our worries and uncertainties of the unknown to widen the gap between acting and focusing our attention on the task at hand, and we end up failing.

You must understand that you are widening the gap when you dwell on the should I or should I not. The bigger the gap gets, the harder it is to bridge it so that you can cross to the other side. You are giving up before you even start, and you can't win with that!

How to close the gap to activate your attention

Reclaim your responsibility

We have mentioned that procrastination widens the gap between attention and action. When you take responsibility for the tasks at hand, your focus shifts from the distraction to what you need to do, the action. This effectually bridges the gap so that you are more accountable, disciplined, and self-aware. It forces you to take stock of your tasks and determine the best course of action. The best trick is to write down your goals or to-do list. This kick-starts your attention and offers you a foundation for the best plan of action. Only then will you develop a methodology to checking the tasks off your list.

Establish a routine

You must realize procrastination is a consistent habit. To be productive, you must set new patterns. Establish a routine that helps you produce reliable results that will make you successful. Control your schedule. What times of the day are you most productive? If you are a morning person, then great! If not, find a schedule that works for you and take charge of it. Over the years, I have found that I am an afternoon-night person. This is the time I focus best. It is the time I find flow.

Finding the time that works for you is not about setting alarms. Instead, it is about dedicating time to your mental and physical well-being: exercising, meditating, and working. It is about building a structure you can stick to while giving you room for self-forgiveness when inevitable hiccups derail your flow.

Share your commitments

When you share your commitment, you become accountable for what you said you would do. You will not put up with anything less or stop until you have completed what you set out to do. Having someone hold you accountable ensures that you are willing and ready to do all it takes to get the intended results. You can also declare your intentions out loud or write them on a sign. Then picture yourself doing it to completion.

Every day, remind yourself of your big WHY. Why it is important and then go ahead and win.

The trick here is to be deliberate with what you say and don't say, what you notice around you, your thoughts, and actions. If your thoughts don't support your goals, replace them with positive thoughts immediately. The whole point here is to channel your attention into everything you intend to do. This way, you close the gap and reign in the resources.

There is no time like the present!

Realize that giving into procrastination does not necessarily mean not accomplishing your goals. It exerts unnecessary emotional and mental stress that affects your life. However, when you choose to take responsibility for your actions, build a routine and structure while focusing your attention and intentions on the tasks at hand, one at a time, you will be empowered to overcome procrastination for good!

Stop worrying

When you are faced by an upsetting situation, it is natural to get worried. However, when you fixate on worry, it can quickly take a toll on your brain and body, hence affecting your focus and decision-making. The human brain has a large pre-frontal cortex that gives it the ability to time travel. In other words, we find ourselves worrying about the future and reflecting on the past. Worry causes us stress, which triggers the brain to secrete stress hormones like adrenaline and cortisol. These hormones play a key role in mobilizing short-term emergency, but when it is prolonged, it can be hazardous. In that state, our attention tends to shift to the cause of worry instead of the task at hand. The memory reshuffles to trigger thoughts relevant to the stress, causing us to slip into bad habits. In short, the neural circuitry responsible for attention is hijacked by worry. When our old habits kick in, our brains begin to shut down, lash out, and ruminate on the past.

So, what can you do to overcome worry and promote focus?

- Write down the whole incident: what happened, how did it happen, what set you off, what did you do, and what would you do differently, given a chance

- Stop what you are doing, focus on your breath, and count to four while inhaling and exhaling

Key Takeaway Points

- Procrastination is the act of putting off tasks to a later time
- The law of the Universe believes there is a lot about our lives we absolutely cannot control
- The only way to defeat procrastination is to know yourself and balance your motivation with your attention
- Pushing yourself too hard when you can't focus will only lower your productivity
- Procrastination has nothing to do with time management, just like it has nothing to do with willpower
- We allow our worries and uncertainties of the unknown to widen the gap between acting and focusing our attention on the task at hand, and we end up failing

- To close the gap, you must:
    - Reclaim your responsibility
    - Establish a routine
    - Share your commitments

Concentrate all your thoughts upon the work in hand. The sun's rays do not burn until brought to a focus

−Alexander Graham Bell.

Chapter 9 The Spiritual Energy Superpower

Spiritual Energy Superpowers

Where were you in 1998? If you are an NBA fan like me, you will remember the 1998 NBA championship finals between Utah Jazz and the Chicago Bulls. Eighteen seconds before the game was up, the Jazz was ahead by one point. There was an invisible shift: Jordan stripped the ball from Malone, slipped away from Byron, and made the winning shot so effortlessly only five seconds to the last whistle. This shot brought the Bulls to their sixth championship, which is considered the greatest play in the NBA sports history.

I still feel like I am at home with my friends and family watching the game like it is happening right now. I still remember what everyone was doing, like most people remember when Neil Armstrong first landed on the moon. As Michael maneuvers with the ball and the clock is ticking, the crowd went silent. We all stood up: our hearts were pounding heavily. The moment becomes the moment for everyone watching: Michael was in the "ZONE!"

The same thing applies to life today – what we are focusing our energy on. Think about it – what happens when you get in the moment–your ZONE?

Know this; your spiritual energy follows attention!

At that moment, you know where you are. You feel like everything is in slow motion, and you start to see things clearly. I bet Michael saw the court very clearly! Even though the Jazz team was trying to block him from taking a shot, he did not focus on the distractions. Instead, he saw right through them to the opportunities right in front of him, and without a question or a whiff of doubt, he took a shot and made one hell of a score!

Think of spiritual energy as your source of life. With it you make your life possible. It refers to the abundant energy flow. You are just a vessel. Spiritual energy simply means to quiet down and feel into yourself and the surroundings. When you feel that animating life force, aura, and intuition within and around you, your energy becomes grounded. You cannot see it but you can feel it. You feel it when you laugh or cry or exist in the present–that is your energy world. It is a neutral force that directs our actions. When you raise your awareness and consciousness, you are choosing to direct your energy toward creativity, connection, and growth. However, when you become less conscious of what is happening within and around you, your energy is directed toward stagnation, separation, and destruction.

Without spiritual energy, your intelligence will be blocked. All the interferences in life stand in the way of the spiritual energy flowing inside you. When you get up in the morning, your spiritual energy starts flowing. As you go through the day and fail to pay attention to the things that matter or fail to trust the process of your life, you invite blockages that prevent the free flow of spiritual energy within.

I like to think of spiritual energy as something you have, and the best part is that you have the power to awaken it. To awaken your spiritual energy, you must let go of the dream world where you sieve everything through ego, rumination of the past, or worrying about the future. What you need is a complete awareness of yourself and then connecting yourself to everything around you.

In other words, you have to quit being an observer and instead ask yourself who is observing!

Perhaps you are thinking, *"How can I dissolve boundaries between myself and my surroundings?"*

To restore your energetic integrity, you must be willing to embark on a journey of self-exploration, taking risks. What are your belief systems? What images do you hold absolute? Restoration can only happen if you take responsibility for the way you use your energy and notice all the places and things that distort your life. As you become conscious and aware of your energy and vibrations, everything in your life begins to fall back into its place—you will know what serves you and what doesn't.

Choosing to stay in the present, by practicing mindfulness, plays a key role in helping us recognize distortions and how to transform them back into their natural state of flow.

Consider this. You are watching a scary murder thriller movie in a movie theater. Your whole being is engrossed in the movie, and the experience feels real. You feel excited, scared, hopeful, and your heart rate is beating fast. Suddenly, someone taps you on the shoulder and you snap back into reality. What was happening? You were fully awakened!

Perhaps you are thinking, *"How do I know that my spiritual energy is awakened?"*

Feeling a sense of connection

We have two minds:

The unconscious mind (also, *the intuitive spirit mind*) operates fast and automatically. It doesn't require much effort or voluntary control. This is what allows you to see the world around you, notice objects, focus attention, fear threats, and avoid losses. It is the place where your emotions, memories, and values are stored to navigate the world around you and make intuitive decisions easily.

The conscious mind (also, *the logical material mind*) analyses and thinks. It requires you to focus your attention to achieve goals deliberately. While this part of the mind is slower, it is more precise–it has unlimited bandwidth. Every task you have on your to-do list is allocated a budget of attention. Going beyond this budget is simply setting yourself up for failure.

These two minds come from a constant and unique interaction between various conflicting psychological forces, hence influencing our behavior and personality.

But how do you use these minds to manifest—turn your dreams into reality—what you want? You must take proactive steps towards your dreams and desires. Nothing happens overnight. Awakening your spiritual energy is a small price to pay to accomplish your goals. In other words, to manifest what you want, you must begin in the energy world to get rid of all the noise and distractions around you. The energy world is unseen, but the material world is seen—and you must have a balanced connection between the two.

Expanding your intuition

Have you ever thought of someone and your phone rings, and it is that someone calling? This is a sign of intuition. Intuition is knowing. Every thought, object, or individual has energy. To experience awakening, you must connect with this energy, and the way to do it is by following your intuition –your gut feeling.

We live in a busy world with so much noise and distractions. To pay attention to your intuition, you must filter out the noise to hear it. Simply slow down and listen. Even a simple act like taking a short walk has the potential to turn up your intuition.

Realize that everything is energy. What you send out to the world always finds its way back. When you smile, you automatically open yourself to positive spiritual energy. However, if you continually send out negative energy, the same energy will find its way back into your life. Shifting your energy to positive things helps you attract more positivity and steers you to realize your goals.

Sometimes, all it takes is to focus your attention on how you want to feel. For instance, if you want to attract more love, your intentions must be set to be more loving. If you want to be more kind, focus your energy on expressing compassion and empathy. That said, you must trust the process. Realize that the process is fluid. All you have to do is quiet the mind, get clarity, and let your intuition speak to you. Allow the energy to flow, notice where it strikes your body, and then let it go!

Manifest synchronicity in life

I like to think of synchronicity as a sign of the Universe telling me my manifestations are on the way.

Have you ever had events happen to you that got you thinking that they are not a coincidence at all? For instance, you have been thinking of buying a Jeep, and for some reason, that day, you meet so many Jeeps on the way, your friend talks about it, you hear it on radio or TV, etc.?

While some people might call this a coincidence, I believe they are subtle signs guiding you. Working with energy creates manifestation. If there are patterns of stuck energy, locate and heal the stuck energy for your manifestations to be successful. Simply open your eyes to everything happening around you: the sounds, nature, smells, people. When you do this, the world will begin to take shape and come alive.

The principle of spiritual energy reminds us of the mind's power and potential.

Remember, the key quality of the mind is to direct attention. You have the power to take charge of your attentive faculties. You choose where to place and hold your attention. To achieve this, you need consistent and intentional mindfulness meditation practice. This will empower the mind to build mental capability to explore our innate gifts and attentions fully. With mindfulness practice, you get up each day to unlimited possibilities of oneness life offers you.

We have mentioned in the previous chapters that the mind can focus and concentrate on one thing and place at a time. With mindfulness, you can train your mind to settle down, be calm and stable. It also opens us to the universal flow of wisdom, experiences our interconnectedness, and embraces our oneness with it.

Whenever you place your attention on something, energy flows. Let's think about this for a second!

When you think of something that happened in the past, recall gratitude for the many blessings we have or difficult experiences we have been through, what happens? A flood of emotions and sensations happens!

Why is that? It is the power of the mind and its attentiveness that help us generate spiritual energy within and create an energy field that influences those around us. Unfortunately, most people are still unaware of the power of attention. We allow ourselves to be pulled and pushed by distractions. Our fears, uncertainties, and painful experiences hold us captive. The energy within us and the energy we send out to the Universe is fragmented, destabilized, and dispersed.

Today, I want you to notice the power of your spiritual energy. Your energy flows where your attention goes and the best opportunity to harness and develop the intrinsic power of attention is by tapping into the five spiritual energy superpowers:

- Mindfulness meditation
- Insight
- Concentration
- Trust
- Right effort

When we do this, we become an energetic force within ourselves and the rest of the world.

Now, let's think of these spiritual superpowers as spokes in a wheel. While they are non-linear, they work together. If you take one away, the wheel will not turn.

If you take away the center or the hub, what you end up with is not a wheel!

The same case applies to these spiritual energy superpowers–they are all interconnected. Our conscious mind possesses these energies, and the best part is that you can cultivate them throughout the day in every task you do. If you are mindful, you possess both insight and attention and generating them lies in the heart of mindfulness meditation practice. They are instrumental in helping you become deeply rooted in every moment of your life.

On the other hand, diligence–the right effort–is the spiritual energy that makes you steadfast in what you do. When you possess a positive state of mind, you boost your cognitive function. Drawing in diligence into your daily tasks, or mindfulness practice, empowers us to cultivate a positive state of mind. But where does trust fit in all these? This is your confidence. I like to look at it as the courage to delve into the unknown with the faith that what lies there makes everything possible.

When you think of mindfulness meditation, what is the first thing that comes to mind?

Most people think meditating is exclusive to yoga gurus on retreat in a serene place, like a forest. However, this is something you and I can do in the comfort of our home or office. Meditation frees the mind from clutter and helps sharpen your attention on tasks that matter most. It has been shown to recharge the brain and put it in a restful/restorative state.

Mindfulness is about raising your sense of awareness without passing judgment on your thoughts, feelings, and sensations and, in other words, focusing your attention on your present moment: thoughts, feelings, actions, surroundings, heartbeat, and breathing. No matter what you choose to focus on, the most important thing is to stay in the *here* and *now* – the present. You can raise your awareness while going about your routine: cleaning, working, reading, walking, jogging, or studying and when your attention is drawn to the present moment, your performance increases.

In a neuroimaging study published in a *Psychiatry Research* journal (2011), researchers measured the brain of 16 people who had never meditated. They were then engaged in a two-month long meditation program where they spent at least 27 minutes practicing mindfulness meditation every day. After the tests, the research participants had increased density of the gray matter in their hippocampus. There was also a significant reduction in the amygdala's size—the part of the brain controlling stress and anxiety. In short, the practice of meditation altered the brain structure and helped improve focus, raise self-awareness, and boost memory.

Mindfulness meditation opens our minds to see things. The brain does not only grow the gray matter but masters how to repair itself organically. It quietens the mind and generates a relaxed feeling that sends signals of happiness to the rest of the body.

But how do you pay attention to your energy?

Listening to your body – what energy feel like and how to tell if the energy is good.

Your body and mind are meant to be whole! To ensure that this happens, your existence is based on a feedback loop. In other words, your body listens to the mind, and the mind listens to the body. The link between the body and mind is awareness. Every cell in your body knows what you are feeling, whether happy, stressed, anxious, etc. The cells' awareness is expressed in the form of neurochemicals and the message it transmits is loud and clear.

Let's consider an example of weight and body image. How you perceive yourself starts in your mind. As your body carries those negative messages from the mind, it mirrors them and the beliefs behind them. So, what can you do to listen to your body?

- You must feel what you feel
- You must accept what you feel
- You must be open to your body

In other words, express willingness to listen. Trust your body, accept that it is spontaneous and value it, and then enjoy what your body wants. Your body likes to be active, and at the same time, it also likes rest. Your body likes different foods, sex, and pleasure. These are the primary things you must focus your attention on. Your body cells feel what it feels and want your body to feel too. The trick here is to learn to listen to what the body's message is. As you allow the layers of denial, self-criticism, and doubt to peel away, you open yourself to the joyful life that lies within.

The basis of self-awareness is allowing yourself to be grounded in your body. Whenever you are distracted, feel your body. If you are driving and someone cuts you off, what do you do? There is a chance you will feel agitated and angry, right? You lose your cool and mutter a few curse words, right? What you are doing is disconnecting yourself from the mind-body field.

Don't allow yourself to be overshadowed by the disruption. Instead, allow yourself to go within to feel your body sensations. Please take a deep breath and use it to bring back your awareness to the present center of focus. Focus on your sensations until they disappear. When you do this, you are cutting out the stimulus-response with an interval of no reaction. In other words, you are stopping the reaction from getting the best of you so that your body is reminded of its natural state of regulation, harmony, and coordination, which ultimately grounds you.

When you allow your reactions to fuel themselves, you get into a state of heightened biological response: elevated heart rate, the release of stress hormones, and hypervigilance. All these are temporary events. They are meant for emergencies only. If you make them a habit, your mind-body field is destabilized and tries to co-exist with the normal state of relaxed awareness and these two don't mix!

When you invite stress and distractions, you are choosing to escape into denial. You cannot drink yourself silly because you are in pain, it will not solve anything. It is only a temporary thing that steals your awareness. You need to stay grounded in your body because that is how you return to a state of wholeness.

Understand that your body is the ultimate messenger of aliveness and bliss. Your body is the vehicle that needs more than just occasional fuel and tune-up. Today, support and celebrate your body by honoring its longings. Find its energizer and comfort. Follow its truth. Trust me, your body has a story to tell, and your part is to enjoy the plot.

What are you training your brain to do?

When you focus your attention on one task at a time, your mind will not drift away into distraction. Your mind becomes clearer and attentive. But this is not always the case. In our minds, we are constantly in a conversation with ourselves. Perhaps you are angry, sad, in love, or fearful. Whatever the emotions attached to your thoughts, you will find yourself in constant dialogue with yourself. No matter how big or small your thoughts are, your body will likely react to them. They change your heart rate, breathing, and hormone-release into the blood circulation. Your emotional response interferes with your thought process and impacts your judgment.

Practicing mindfulness meditation allows you to watch your thoughts and emotions come and go without passing judgment. In other words, your body's response is no longer part of the equation, hence calming your mind.

There are three things you must do when practicing mindfulness meditation:

- Slow down. Watch your thoughts come and go like the ocean tides
- Notice everything happening around you as though they are happening for the first time
- No matter what you do, do it perfectly. When you do small tasks perfectly, you start realizing how easy it is to do large and complex tasks, too. In other words, your attention is drawn to everything you do without getting distracted by useless mind chatter

Exercise

As you go about your tasks, raise your awareness of your breathing. Widen your focus to include your bodily sensations, thoughts, and feelings. Focus your mind on the task at hand. When you notice your mind drift away, watch those thoughts come and go without judging. Then gently pull back your attention to the task at hand.

Check-in with your body from time to time. Appreciate your head, eyes, nose, mouth, jaw, and tongue. Drop your jaw and appreciate how it feels like when you are relaxed. Notice the words, stories, movements, and sounds that reside in your head. Feel the weight of your head and how it feels on your shoulders. Appreciate what your mind has helped you figure out in this world.

Next, go to your neck and throat and notice if it has lumps and gasps of freedom. Think of what a balanced neck would look and feel like. Move to your chest and notice all the emotions it embodies. When you inhale deep into your chest, what images arise from there? Are there burdens, memories, and images you have been carrying on your chest? Is there a song or rhythm there? What's the story?

Think about your shoulders and the responsibilities it carries. Breathe deep into that area and feel the airflow through into the hands. What movements want to happen? The deaf use their hands to tell a story—what story do your hands tell? Appreciate them for serving you so graciously.

Check in with your gut and appreciate how much space it occupies on your body. This is where your power rests. Touch your belly button and think of yourself as a baby—this is where your development started. This is where you were attached to your mother. It is where you got life. Breathe in and out of your belly and notice the rhythm, fear, and its story of strength.

Take your attention to your hips and imagine them moving sensually as though you were dancing salsa. Feel the movement's potential power and allow yourself to connect the lower body with the upper body. What story resides here? Slowly bring your attention to your thighs and knees—feel the supportive connection. Feel the flow of energy from your feet up to your head. Imagine your legs like tree trunks and think about the kind of trees they would be—sturdy, strong, and well-developed. Appreciate the work they do.

Finally, travel to your knees and appreciate their roles—flight and jump. Imagine wearing tight shoes and appreciate how they fight back to take care of you. What story do your feet carry—the dancing, the jumping, running, etc. What would your feet want from you right now? Have you neglected them? Appreciate what it does to carry your whole body: its connectedness to the ground to support you as you walk, dance, shake from fear, and jump with joy, and allow yourself to rest on that solid ground.

Key Takeaway Points

- Spiritual energy is something you have, and the best part is that you have the power to awaken it
- To awaken your spiritual energy, you must let go of the dream world where you sieve everything through ego, rumination of the past, or worrying about the future
- What you send out to the world always finds its way back
- Quiet the mind, get clarity, and let your intuition speak to you
- The principle of spiritual energy reminds us of the mind's power and potential
- You have the power to take charge of your attentive faculties. You choose where to place and hold your attention
- Whenever you place your attention on something, energy flows
- The intrinsic power of attention is obtained by tapping into the five spiritual energy superpowers:
    - Mindfulness meditation
    - Insight
    - Concentration

- o   Trust
- o   Right effort
- Mindfulness is about raising your sense of awareness without passing judgment on your thoughts, feelings, and sensations and, in other words, focusing your attention on your present moment: thoughts, feelings, actions, surroundings, heartbeat, and breathing
- Your body and mind are meant to be whole!
- Trust your body, accept that it is spontaneous and value it, and then enjoy what your body wants
- The basis of self-awareness is allowing yourself to be grounded in your body

Completeness and unity constitute our most fundamental nature as living beings. That is true for all of us. No matter how wonderful or terrible our lives have been, no matter how many traumas and scars we may carry from the past, no matter what we have gone through or what we are suffering now, our intrinsic wholeness is always present, and we can recognize it

−Sharon Salzberg.

Chapter 10 Behavioral Learning

Learning Toolbox

Have you thought of any new skills to learn?

Is all behavior learned through the environment? Let's go back to the story of our most exceptional cat who observed her master teach children to play piano and developed this exceptional skill. After keen observation, she perched herself up at the piano and started tapping the keys with her paws, just like the children did. Is there a difference in learning behavior between humans and animals?

Behaviorism mainly focuses on changes in our observable behavior, what we say and do. When it comes to learning how to drive, where is your focus? Is it on doing the driving or explaining how to drive? If you are learning how to cook, are you most focused on explaining the recipe and cooking procedures or producing the kitchen's actual food? During training, are you focused on teaching or reflecting on what you are doing in the middle of the training session?

Behaviorism theory states that all behaviors are learned through our interaction with the environment, and innate factors have very little influence on our behaviors. I like to think of behaviorism as a form of positive reinforcement—if a student scores 90% and above in their math test, they get a small treat. In that case, students work even harder in the future tests to get the reward, otherwise termed as operant conditioning.

According to Ivan Pavlov, a Russian psychologist (1998), he researched dog salivation in food response. Whenever the dogs would hear a bell ring, they would be given food. After a while, the bell would ring, and the dogs would start salivating because they expected food even before they could see it. This is what behaviorism means—our experiences and environment are the key drivers of our actions—otherwise termed classical conditioning.

We all want to improve our productivity by focusing our attention on things that matter most. We have seen that time is constant and has no bearing on how productive you are at work. To get ahead, you must be willing to improve yourself. Now that you know you want to be better at how you focus your attention, how do you do it?

Mastering a new skill is paramount in today's world. To stay competitive, you must be willing to learn new skills. It is not enough to be smart. You must seek out opportunities to be smarter every day. You must stretch yourself even if it gets uncomfortable. To get started:

Check how ready you are

When developing a new skill, you must ask yourself whether the goal is attainable and how much energy you can give to the project. There is a limit to what you can learn. Learning to focus your attention is not the same as refilling your meds at the pharmacy. Improving yourself takes hard work. It does not mean that you cannot master a new skill—that is rubbish! You must recognize that learning new skills takes commitment. Unless you make your goal attainable and are ready to work at it, you will not get anywhere!

Is it required?

Is a new skill you want to learn relevant to what you are doing? If you don't value what you are trying to learn, then it will never work. Realize that learning a new skill is an investment of your energy and time, and the most important thing is to know what the return will be when you have it.

How best do you learn?

As we have mentioned, learning a new behavior can be observational, through reward or a stimulus. The question is, how best do you learn? Look back at all the skills you have acquired in the past and ask yourself how you learned them. What was your learning style? Are you a visual, auditory, reading/writing, kinesthetic learner or do you have a combination of two or more learning styles? This will help you determine the learning environment that works best for you.

Get the right support

Getting the right help can greatly impact your learning. Look around you—is there someone who has mastered the new skill you are trying to master? It doesn't have to be someone that is immediately close to you. The most important thing is that they will notice the change in your behavior and give you honest feedback. Ultimately, you want to pick the right support – one that will give you quality mentorship.

Start small

When learning a new skill, it is easy to feel overwhelmed. In the beginning, you will want to take on everything, resulting in burnout. The most important thing is to choose one skill to focus on, one at a time. Then break your goal into manageable bite-size mini-goals you can take on. Remember, if you do the right activities you will get the right results.

Then reflect along the way. As you move from the experimental stage to mastery, think about what you have learned to make it stick. You want to surround yourself with people who can offer you both informational and emotional support every step of the way. They don't have to have everything figured out, as long as they can give you honest feedback on your progress. When you share your progress with your support system, you don't only get valuable feedback but also become accountable and cement the behavioral change.

Finally, exercise patience. You will not nail it at first, but you must keep trying. It takes even longer to make a new skill ingrained in your system. It even takes longer for people around you to notice the behavior change and that is okay. Take baby steps, and before you know it, you will be there! Progress = happiness.

Skills you can learn to improve your productivity

Boundary setting
Imagine this. You just got back to the office from vacation and tried to catch up with project progress and ways forward. However, your colleagues and team members are knocking at your door one after the other to say hello and probably catch up on the juicy details of your adventures.

While these interruptions are not a problem as they allow you to connect, collaborate, and promote work dynamics, they can leave you frustrated and completely drained. The more you focus your attention on the distraction, the further your attention falls behind from what matters most—project progress.

The trick is to set boundaries that best serve your purpose. When you know who and what demands your attention, you can correlate those demands to the window of opportunity as much as you can to boost productivity, retain your sanity while promoting goodwill in the process. These strategies will help you achieve that:

Communicate your needs, goals, and limits

You cannot be available for everyone and everything at all times. There will be times when you must turn down your involvement to avoid compromising your energy in other forms. You must learn to prioritize demands to make better decisions about where, when, and how to spend your energy on tasks that will bring you closer to your goals. People don't have to agree with your choices all the time, but you need to let them know what you can and cannot do and when your attention needs to be focused on the most important things on your to-do list.

Have an open mind

Most of the time, we want to be available to everyone that needs us, and hence keep our doors open to them. On the surface, this might seem to work, but it will not serve your best interests. While we may not foresee every responsibility that comes our way, you can let people know when they can have your undivided attention.

Expressing your open-mindedness allows people to know when you are physically attentive and intellectually and emotionally attentive. When you carve out boundaries, you make it possible to turn off your phone, shut the door, or decline drop-ins to work on tasks that require your full attention.

Prioritize the tasks at hand

It is not enough to allocate time to the people and projects that need our attention—but it is a good start. It is necessary to stop multitasking! While the brain can receive many stimuli simultaneously, it can only process stimuli that are related. A major source of problems is allowing our attention to be pulled in different directions by various tasks. Multitasking makes it hard to filter irrelevancy and, manage working memory, and you become chronically distracted.

However, by establishing tangible boundaries, you are better placed to concentrate on one task at a time. This way, you can achieve more than you could when you spread your attention across multiple tasks.

When you decide to focus your attention on the task at hand, you can move on to others when you are done, without feelings of guilt. Unless you establish tangible boundaries, certain tasks and relationships risk expanding to take up the energy we give them and demand even more. For instance, when you respond instantaneously to every email, text, or call that comes through, you teach people to depend on you all the time. As these demands ooze into what matters most, the boundaries get blurry and we lose sight of our priorities and how to achieve them when everything else is screaming for our attention.

When we set boundaries, we teach others to view us as valuable resources and training ourselves to be available to tasks and people who need us most.

Reciprocate

You cannot expect people to respect your boundaries when you don't give a damn about their boundaries. When people ask to reschedule or turn down projects we assign them, it is not a license to guilt them into doing what we ask them to. While it may be inconvenient, our role is to elevate others to succeed in the best ways they have defined for themselves.

Decision-making

We all make decisions every day, but how many of us can say we are decisive enough in ways that help us be more productive and successful in what we do?

There are times when we are called upon to make tough decisions, but how many make them? Or do we avoid them altogether? To be more productive in your tasks, you must make tough decisions fast, accurately, and with a great degree of confidence. You must know where you are going first for you to make effective decisions.

Ask yourself:

- Are my goals clear?
- Do I have a clear why?
- Do I possess a clear risk perspective?
- Am I asking the right questions? Are my reasons aligned?

Once you have all these approaches in place, you are ready to start making decisions. This will not happen overnight. You must be willing to train yourself to practice as much as possible until you can make better, accurate, and productive decisions–faster than you have ever made them before.

Delegating

Do you know whether the tasks you have on your to-do list are important, urgent, or not? Not everything on your to-do list demands your attention. According to the Eisenhower's Decision principle, there is a difference between what is important and what is not; what is urgent and what is not urgent.

Let's take a look at the Eisenhower's Decision Matrix. The matrix helps you decide what is or isn't important or urgent. There are four quadrants in this matrix:

Quadrant 1	Quadrant 2
Important and urgent	Important but not urgent
Quadrant 3	**Quadrant 4**
Not important but urgent	Not important and not urgent

Quadrant 1 = Important and urgent tasks

Quadrant 2 = Important but not urgent tasks

Quadrant 3 = Not important but urgent

Quadrant 4 = Not important and not urgent

Quadrant 1 consists of tasks that require your immediate attention and you must work on eliminating them with priority. These are tasks that work toward satisfying your purpose in life. Typically, they are problems, deadlines, and crises.

Quadrant 2 consists of tasks that don't necessarily have short deadlines, but they are key to helping you achieve important goals. Typically, they are the tasks that strengthen your relationships, help you plan the future, and achieve personal growth. This is where we should spend most of our time because these tasks hold the key to lasting happiness, satisfaction, and success.

Quadrant 3 consists of tasks that require our immediate attention, but they don't necessarily steer us toward our goals and life's purpose. However, they help others achieve their goals. Unfortunately, most people confuse Quadrant 3 and Quadrant 1. While these tasks are important to others, they are not that important to you. Spending too much focus on these tasks tends to leave people feeling like they have done a lot of work but have not made progress towards achieving their goals—which leaves them frustrated and resentful. The trick here is to be more assertive, firm yet polite when turning down requests.

Quadrant 4 consists of distractions – nothing important nor urgent. These tasks don't help you achieve your goals in any way. While you can delete most of the tasks on this category, they are key to helping the brain decompress at the end of a hectic day.

In short, the activities on Quadrant 1 require action, Quadrant 2 requires you to decide what needs to be done, Quadrant 3 can be delegated, and you can avoid or delete Quadrant 4 altogether.

So, what is delegating?

Delegating means matching tasks with specific employees who have the right skill set for the task so that you are free to accomplish other more important activities. As a leader, your responsibility is to seek growth and expansion continually. However, when you are heavily involved in an endless list of tasks, it can be impossible to grow. If a long list of tasks weighs you down, it is almost impossible to focus your attention and energy on the vision of growing your business or career.

While the process of delegating is complex and at times requires trial and error, it plays a key role in boosting your level of productivity. The technique you need to master is to learn how, when, and who to delegate to. The best strategy to delegate:

- Select the right person for the job
- Explain to them why you are delegating
- Offer the right instructions and guidance
- Give them relevant resources and training for the job
- Give them authority to take on the task
- Follow up and give feedback

Goal setting

Do you have a goal? Do you consider yourself goal-less or goal-obsessed?

A goal is an object of your effort. It is your desired outcome. It is the place you want to be once you complete several tasks. Unfortunately, there are people without goals who just drift through life without being happy or knowing why. Others are goal-obsessed: they go around always stressed out and unhappy even when they achieve material success.

Setting goals is not about defining a direction for your life. Instead, it is about giving you milestones to derive satisfaction during the journey and once you achieve them. One route to boosting your productivity is by setting:

- Clearly defined goals
- Realistic goals
- Challenging goals
- Meaningful goals

Once you meet the criteria above, the next thing is to write your goals on a piece of paper, determine the tasks that need to be completed to achieve the goal, set deadlines for those tasks, and then expend your attention and energy on tasks that have defined.

Key Takeaway Points

- Behaviorism mainly focuses on changes in our observable behavior: what we say and do
- All behaviors are learned through our interaction with the environment, and innate factors have very little influence on our behaviors
- To stay competitive, you must be willing to learn new skills. It is not enough to be smart. You must seek out opportunities to be smarter every day

- Unless you make your goal attainable and are ready to work at it, you will not get anywhere
- Learning a new skill is an investment of your energy and time, and the most important thing is to know what the return will be when you have it
- Break your goal into manageable bite-size mini-goals you can take on
- It takes longer to make a new skill ingrained in your system. It takes even longer for people around you to notice the behavior change. Take baby steps, and before you know it, you will reach your goal
- Set boundaries that best serve your purpose
- When you know who and what demands your attention, you can correlate those demands to the window of opportunity as much as you can to boost productivity, retain your sanity while promoting goodwill in the process
- Setting goals is not about defining a direction for your life – it is about giving you milestones to derive satisfaction during the journey and once you achieve them

Life is hard. Life is difficult. Life is going to punch you in the gut. But when you change your attitude, you change your behavior. When your behavior changes, so do your results

–Will Hurd.

Chapter 11 Instilling Good Habits

Force of Habit

I read the story of two tadpoles: Ted and Todd. These tadpoles hatched from the same batch of eggs and always swam with great enthusiasm. They would swim up to their mother shouting with excitement, "Look at what we can do and why we can!" Their mother looked at them with so much pride and explained that they would eventually lose their tail and, instead, grow legs. You would think that the tadpoles would be saddened by the news, right?

But not Ted. On hearing the news, he got excited about the future. He kept swimming with so much vibrancy and enthusiasm, occasionally checking if his legs had started forming. He kept strengthening his tail and built stamina. On the other hand, Todd did not see the point of exercising a tail that would eventually drop off —his energy dropped, and the tail grew weaker as the days went by.

After a while, their tails dropped off, and they started growing legs. Ted was full of excitement, and his energy never died down. While Todd was happy he had legs, he did not have the energy to use his legs. He had developed a habit of just getting by.

What habits have you learned?

Sometimes, I hear people saying, "I don't see how learning science is helping me in life today." What they fail to realize is that learning in and by itself is a skill. Realize that the life you have right now is the sum of your habits. Whether you are in shape or not, it results from all the habits you have instilled over the years.

What you repeatedly do becomes who you are: your beliefs, values, and overall personality. The next time you are tempted to think, "*What is the point?*" remember the story of Ted and Todd.

Habits are behaviors we repeatedly have and have become ingrained in our subconscious. Formation of habits involve four steps:

- **Cue:** Cue triggers the brain to engage in the behavior. If you look around you, you will realize that most of the time, you are picking up cues that will earn you a secondary reward: power, fame, money, approval, love, or personal satisfaction. The mind is constantly analyzing the internal and external environment for clues of where rewards are located. When you see a cue, you know a reward is right around the corner

- **Craving:** Once you find a cue, you start craving for the reward. This is your motivation to act. Without it, you have no reason to act. This is not the habit itself but the feeling it brings. For instance, when you smoke, you don't crave the cigarette but the relief it brings. You brush your teeth because you crave the feeling of a clean mouth and fresh breath. In other words, the craving you have is associated with a desire to change your inner state
    - Cravings differ from one person to another. We are not all motivated by the same cues. Your cue is nothing if it is not interpreted. Your thoughts and emotions transform your cravings

- **Response:** Response is the actual habit performed. It can be a thought or an action. For a response to happen, you must be motivated enough to expend the required mental effort

- **Reward**: Reward is the end goal of a habit. Your cue notices the reward, and you begin to crave it. Your response is how to obtain the reward, and you begin to chase it for satisfaction and lessons. Perhaps you craved a promotion for the reward of money and respect. Understand that your brain detects the reward and is constantly monitoring actions that deliver pleasure

What if behavior is insufficient in any of the steps? In that case, it doesn't become a habit. When you get rid of the cue, reduce the craving, make the behavior complex, or have an unsatisfying reward, you will never develop a habit. In other words, without one, you have no behavior, and without all four, your behavior will not be repeated!

Think about this—when your phone buzzes with a text message, you crave to know the content of the text, and so you grab the phone to read it. In that instance, grabbing the phone is associated with reading a text. When you get up in the morning, you want to stay alert, so you prepare a cup of coffee. Drinking coffee becomes associated with getting up.

Perhaps you don't even realize the habits that run your life and whether they are good or bad. If you think about the things, you do each morning–tying your shoes, making a cup of coffee, unplugging the coffee maker after use, changing clothes once we get home– why do you think you do them?

After years of repeated habits and mental programming, our patterns of thinking and acting become automatic. Similarly, if you want to get things done, you must pair your craving with habits that support and deliver your desire.

How many times have you heard people say, "I can't seem to concentrate for long!"

Many, right?

Most people assume that attention is something we have or don't have. However, attention is something you do. When you can't focus on tasks, you are not devoted to focusing beyond what your natural tendencies allowed. You have not practiced focusing your attention.

But how can you develop this habit?

Limit technology

We live in a world that is driven by technology. Everywhere you turn, people are either on their phones, iPads, or computers. The biggest downside to technology is addiction. Technology has become part of our lives such that no one can take them away from us. Unfortunately, technology steals your attention from the things that matter most. You are always tempted to check what gossip is happening on social media, what notifications you have, or who is saying what, when, and where. By limiting the use of technology, much of your attention will shift to the most important things of sleep and tasks at hand, both of which leave you more productive.

Determine when you are most productive

What time of the day are you most productive?

For most people, morning routines play a key role in developing a new habit. For instance, the 20/20/20 rule requires that when you first get up in the morning, you divide the first hour into 20 minutes of movements, 20 minutes of self-reflection, and 20 minutes of growth/self-improvement.

Knowing the time you are most productive helps you schedule tasks to that time of the day, making it easier to focus your full attention on accomplishing them with little or no distractions. The most important thing is to structure your schedule to fit the most active parts of your day so that your potential to deliver is optimal.

Adding on a simple act of chewing gum has also been shown by the *British Journal of Psychology* (2013) to help one focus longer, especially when working on tasks requiring close monitoring. This is because chewing gum increases the flow of blood to the brain, which in turn sparks learning, mood, intelligence, and memory.

Break tasks into bite-size chunks

Success is a few simple disciplines, practiced every day; while failure is simply a few errors in judgment, repeated every day

–Jim Rohn.

When building new habits, it helps to start small so that it is easy to say no. You don't need willpower or more motivation to get things done. Researchers at Columbia University–IDEA Fitness Journal, 2008– revealed that willpower works like a muscle. As you use it throughout the day, it gets fatigued. To instill a good habit, you start small and build up your momentum little by little.

If you want to lose weight, it is easy to start with five pushups and build up to 50 pushups per day instead of jumping right into the deep end. The point is to make it easy enough to get tasks done without motivation.

As you begin to build up, break the habit into bite-size chunks. This will help you maintain the momentum and make the behavior easy to accomplish. That said, always finish what you start.

Key Takeaway Points

- Habits are behaviors we repeatedly have and have become ingrained in our subconscious
- Formation of habits involve four steps:
    - Cue
    - Craving
    - Response
    - Reward
- Attention is not something we have, or don't have – it is something we do
- Limiting the use of technology, much of your attention will shift to the most important things
- Structure your schedule to fit the most active parts of your day so that your potential to deliver is optimal

- Break habits into bite-size chunks to help you maintain the momentum and make the behavior easy to accomplish
- Finish what you start
- A simple act of chewing gum helps one focus longer, especially when working on tasks requiring close monitoring. This is because chewing gum increases the flow of blood to the brain, which in turn sparks learning, mood, intelligence, and memory
- 20 minutes of exercise, 20 minutes journaling, 20 minutes learning and self-improvement will increase attention, mindfulness, and performance

Habit is the intersection of knowledge (what to do),
skill (how to do),
and desire (want to do).

—Stephen R. Covey.

Conclusion

I heard an old Zen story of a student and their master. The student asked the master to write them something of great wisdom, and the master picked up a brush and wrote the word, "Attention." The student asked their master, "Is that it?" The master picked up the brush and wrote, "Attention. Attention." Agitated, the student asked, "That doesn't make any sense to me." Again, the master picked up and brush and wrote, "Attention. Attention. Attention!" The student was a little confused, and so he asked his master what the word means. The master's response was, "Attention is attention!"

We have discussed so much about attention, and from what we have gathered, attention is the secret of life. Often when asked to pay attention to what matters most, we don't see anything exciting about it. We assume that attention is boring. Instead of raising awareness of the simple things we do every day, we struggle to attach importance. Every moment we live, and everything we do in life is absolute!

In other words, there is no better time than the present! When we fail to focus our attention on the little things we do, we miss the point. It can be meditating, chopping onions, dicing tomatoes, peeling potatoes, cleaning the house, or catching up with our children after a long day. It does not matter what the content of the *present* is because every moment is absolute! If only you could pay attention to the things you do, you would never have to procrastinate, get frustrated, stressed, and out of balance.

The problem arises when we bring our self-centered thoughts to the *present* all day long. In other words, when attention shifts from the present moment, you create a gap in your awareness of reality. Into that gap flows all kinds of life's mischief, and the gap keeps expanding day after day. You keep telling yourself, "I must have it my way!"

The whole point of focusing our attention on the things that matter most is to close this gap. This way, you don't have to spend your energy and effort on self-centered thoughts. When you raise your awareness of everything that matters—the present—no gap or space arises. Whenever you get self-centered thoughts telling you to do something else—more pleasurable—you know there is a gap. Whenever you complain about your goals, you are in a gap.

It doesn't matter how much time you have or what time of day it is. If you don't focus your attention on the tasks at hand, time will not add any value. Realize that attention goes beyond completing a task. Attention shapes your frame of life—your bigger picture. By just looking at what you pay attention to, you can tell what you value most; that is what molds your soul and character. Your focus becomes your reality. This is why you must actively and intentionally shift your attention away from distractions to your life's purpose. You are the supreme commander of your mind. You must know why you are fighting this battle to have a plan for how to attain victory.

To increase your ability to manage your attention, you must define the level of control and attention a task, experience, or moment requires. While this may depend on the nature of work you do and your life's priorities, finding the right mix that works best for you is instrumental in helping you take back control of your attention, be more present, and leverage your inner genius. This way, you will live a life you choose and not one of reaction and distraction.

The ball is on your court—what do you want to do?

The universe is saying to you today:
Where you focus your attention
is what will present in your life.
Life is a mirror and
it reflects back to you what you project.
Keep moving forward and trust yourself more

—Healing Energy Tools.

If my book helped you in any way, be it guidance for yourself, for a friend, or even if it taught you something about attention management, make sure to leave it a review! Thank you for reading, and I wish you all the best!

Felicity

Bibliography

Baldauf, D., & Desimone, R. (2014). "Neural mechanisms of object-based attention", *Science,* 344(6182), 424-427.

Bonnet, M. H., & Arand, D. L. (2003). "Clinical effects of sleep fragmentation versus sleep deprivation". *Sleep medicine reviews,* 7(4), 297-310.

Covey, S. (2011). *The 7 habits of highly effective teens.* Simon and Schuster.

Erickson, K. I., Voss, M. W., Prakash, R. S., Basak, C., Szabo, A., Chaddock, L., ... & Kramer, A. F. (2011). "Exercise training increases size of hippocampus and improves memory". *Proceedings of the National Academy of Sciences,* 108(7), 3017-3022.

Ferriss, T. (2007). The Not-To-Do List: 9 Habits to Stop Now. Retrieved 19 March 2021, from https://tim.blog/2007/08/16/the-not-to-do-list-9-habits-to-stop-now/

Freud, S. (1899). *The interpretation of dreams,* trans. J. Crick. Oxford University Press.(Original work published in 1899.)[SL].

Gomez-Pinilla, F., & Hillman, C. (2013). "The influence of exercise on cognitive abilities". *Comprehensive Physiology, 3*(1), 403-428.

Hölzel, B. K., Carmody, J., Vangel, M., Congleton, C., Yerramsetti, S. M., Gard, T., & Lazar, S. W. (2011). "Mindfulness practice leads to increases in regional brain gray matter density". *Psychiatry research: neuroimaging,* 191(1), 36-43.

https://www.cnbc.com/2017/10/06/tony-robbins-this-is-the-secret-to-happiness-in-one-word.html.

James, W. (2007). *The principles of psychology* (Vol. 1). Cosimo, Inc.

Lamport, D. J., Chadwick, H. K., Dye, L., Mansfield, M. W., & Lawton, C. L. (2014). "A low glycemic load breakfast can attenuate cognitive impairments observed in middle aged obese females with impaired glucose tolerance". *Nutrition, Metabolism and Cardiovascular Diseases,* 24(10), 1128-1136.

Leslie Mann, S. (2013). "Study finds nearly half of Americans not drinking enough water". https://www.chicagotribune.com/lifestyles/ct-xpm-2013-06-05-ct-x-0605-drinking-water-20130605-story.html

Levitin, Daniel J. (2015-09-23). "Why It's So Hard to Pay Attention, Explained By Science". Fast Company. Retrieved 2020-04-09.

Mark, G., Gudith, D., & Klocke, U. (2008, April). "The cost of interrupted work: more speed and stress". In Proceedings of the SIGCHI conference on Human Factors in Computing Systems (pp. 107-110).

McGonigal, K. (2008). "The science of willpower: research supports the notion that willpower works like a muscle--so how do you train it?" *IDEA Fitness Journal*, 5(6), 42-50.

Milstein, J. A., Dalley, J. W., & Robbins, T. W. (2005). "Neuropharmacology of Attention". In *Neurobiology of Attention* (pp. 57-62). Academic Press.

Morgan, K., Johnson, A. J., & Miles, C. (2014). "Chewing gum moderates the vigilance decrement". *British Journal of Psychology*, 105(2), 214-225.

Nelson, C. A. (2008). "Incidental findings in magnetic resonance imaging (MRI) brain research". *The Journal of Law, Medicine & Ethics*, 36(2), 315-319.

Newport, C. (2016). *Deep work: Rules for focused success in a distracted world*. Hachette UK.

Peters, R. (2006). "Ageing and the brain". *Postgraduate medical journal*, 82(964), 84-88.

Sperry, R. W. (1967). "Split-brain approach to learning problems". *The neu.*

Tefft BC, AAA Foundation for Traffic Safety. Prevalence of Motor Vehicle Crashes Involving Drowsy Drivers, United States, 2009 – 2013 [457 KB].Washington, DC: AAA Foundation for Traffic Safety; 2014. October 19, 2015.

Wittbrodt, M. T., & Millard-Stafford, M. (2018). "Dehydration impairs cognitive performance: a meta-analysis". *Med Sci Sports Exerc*, 50(11), 2360-2368.

Yoo, S. S., Hu, P. T., Gujar, N., Jolesz, F. A., & Walker, M. P. (2007). "A deficit in the ability to form new human memories without sleep". *Nature neuroscience,* 10(3), 385-392.

www.ingramcontent.com/pod-product-compliance
Lightning Source LLC
Chambersburg PA
CBHW052349220526
45465CB00003BA/1028